SCOTT FORESMAN • ADDISON WESLEY

Mathematics

Grade 2

Practice Masters/Workbook

Editorial Offices: Glenview, Illinois • Parsippany, New Jersey • New York, New York

Sales Offices: Parsippany, New Jersey • Duluth, Georgia • Glenview, Illinois
Coppell, Texas • Ontario, California • Mesa, Arizona

Overview

Practice Masters/Workbook provides additional practice on the concept or concepts taught in each lesson.

ISBN 0-328-04954-9

Copyright © Pearson Education, Inc.
All Rights Reserved. Printed in the United States of America. This publication, or parts thereof, may be used with appropriate equipment to reproduce copies for classroom use only.

13 14 15 V084 09 08

Name _____

Joining Groups to Add

P 1-1

Count the fruit in the two groups.
Draw and write how many there are in all.

1.

   __4__ and __3__ is __7__ in all.

2.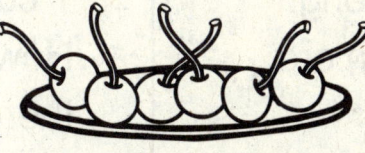

   ____ and ____ is ____ in all.

3.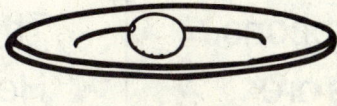

   ____ and ____ is ____ in all.

Problem Solving *Algebra*

4. Draw the number of missing apples.
   Write the missing number.

    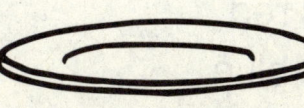 

   5 and ____ is ____ in all.

Use with Lesson 1-1.

Name _____

Writing Addition Sentences

P 1-2

Write an addition sentence to solve the problem.

1. 5 boys are at the party.
   6 girls are at the party.
   How many children are there in all?

   __5__ + __6__ = __11__ children

2. There are 6 blue hats.
   There are 2 red hats.
   How many hats are there in all?

   _____ + _____ = _____ hats

3. 4 children play a game.
   5 children sing a song.
   How many children are there in all?

   _____ + _____ = _____ children

4. 7 cups are on the table.
   1 cup is on a shelf.
   How many cups are there in all?

   _____ + _____ = _____ cups

5. There are 3 red ribbons.
   There are 3 blue ribbons.
   How many ribbons are there in all?

   _____ + _____ = _____ ribbons

6. There are 7 gifts for Suzi.
   There are 0 gifts for David.
   How many gifts are there in all?

   _____ + _____ = _____ gifts

Problem Solving *Visual Thinking*

Complete the addition sentence.

7. There are 7 balloons in all.
   Color some balloons red.
   Color some balloons blue.

   _____ + _____ = _____ balloons

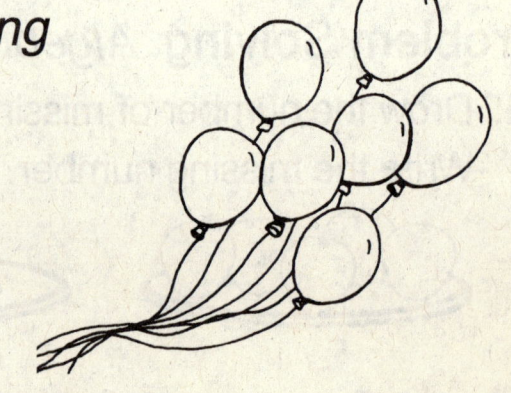

2   Use with Lesson 1-2.

Name _____

PROBLEM-SOLVING STRATEGY   P 1-3
Write a Number Sentence

Write a number sentence to solve the problem.

1. 6 goldfish are in one bowl.
   4 goldfish are in another bowl.
   How many goldfish are there altogether?

   _6_ ⊕ _4_ ⊜ _10_ goldfish

2. There are 3 mice in a cage.
   There are 4 mice in another cage.
   How many mice are there in all?

   ____ ◯ ____ ◯ ____ mice

3. There are 2 frogs on a rock.
   There are 6 frogs in the water.
   How many frogs are there in all?

   ____ ◯ ____ ◯ ____ frogs

4. 3 kittens are playing.
   8 kittens are sleeping.
   How many kittens are there in all?

   ____ ◯ ____ ◯ ____ kittens

5. 5 butterflies are on a flower.
   4 butterflies are on another flower.
   How many butterflies are there in all?

   ____ ◯ ____ ◯ ____ butterflies

Use with Lesson 1-3.   **3**

Taking Away to Subtract

P 1-4

Write the numbers.

1. ___ 6 ___

2. ___ 7 ___

9 take away 3 is 6.

11 take away 4 is 7.

3. 7 take away 1 is ___.

4. 5 take away 0 is ___.

5. 6 take away 2 is ___.

6. 8 take away 7 is ___.

7. 9 take away 4 is ___.

8. 7 take away 4 is ___.

9. 10 take away 3 is ___.

10. 8 take away 0 is ___.

Problem Solving *Algebra*

Circle the pennies that answer the question.

7. Beth started with 5 pennies. She lost 2 pennies. How many pennies does Beth now have?

4 Use with Lesson 1-4.

Name _____

PROBLEM-SOLVING SKILL   P 1-7

Choose an Operation

Circle **add** or **subtract**.
Then write the number sentence to solve the problem.

1. Sasha has 12 toy cars. She gives 6 of them to Michael. How many toy cars does Sasha have left?   add   (subtract)

   12 ⊖ 6 ◯ 6 ___ toy cars

2. Sara has 7 crayons. Bobby gives her 1 more crayon. How many crayons does Sara have in all?   add   subtract

   ___ ◯ ___ ◯ ___ crayons

3. 8 children play a game. 4 children go home. How many children are left playing the game?   add   subtract

   ___ ◯ ___ ◯ ___ children

4. 5 children play hopscotch. 3 children play jump rope. How many more children play hopscotch?   add   subtract

   ___ ◯ ___ ◯ ___ children

Reasoning *Writing in Math*

5. Write a math story. Then write a number sentence to solve it.

   _____

   _____

   _____

Use with Lesson 1-7. **7**

Name _____

Adding in Any Order

P 1-8

Write the sum. Then write the related addition fact.

1. $2 + 4 = \underline{6}$

   $\underline{4} + \underline{2} = \underline{6}$

2. $7 + 1 = \underline{}$

   _____

3. $9 + 2 = \underline{}$

   _____

4. $5 + 3 = \underline{}$

   _____

5.
```
    6
  + 4
  ___
```
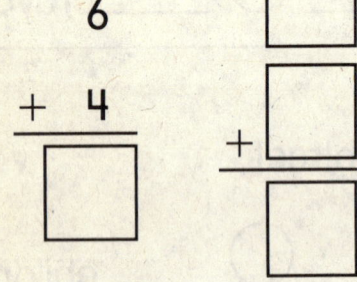

6.
```
    3
  + 4
  ___
```
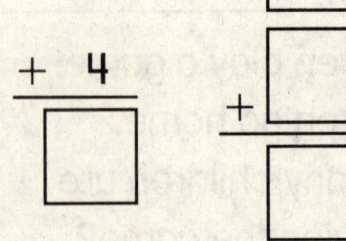

Problem Solving *Writing in Math*

Write a number sentence to solve the problem.

7. There are 4 birds in the nest. 3 birds join them. How many birds are there in all?

   ____ ◯ ____ ◯ ____ birds

8. Change the order of the addends in the number sentence in Exercise 7. Write a story for this new number sentence.

   _____

   _____

Use with Lesson 1-8.

Ways to Make 10

Find different ways to make 10.
Complete each number sentence.

1. 5 + __5__ = 10
2. ____ + 2 = 10
3. 9 + ____ = 10
4. 10 = ____ + 7
5. 4 + ____ = 10
6. 10 = 10 + ____

Write five more ways to make 10. Use different number sentences from those in Exercises 1–6.

7. ____ + ____ = 10
8. ____ + ____ = 10
9. ____ + ____ = 10
10. ____ + ____ = 10
11. ____ + ____ = 10

Problem Solving Mental Math

Use mental math to find the missing numbers.
Look for the pattern in each chart.

12. Make 8

0	1	2	3	4
				4

13. Make 6

0		
6		

Fact Families

Complete each fact family.

1. $8 + 2 = 10$
   $2 + 8 = 10$
   ___ − ___ = ___
   ___ − ___ = ___

2. ___ + ___ = ___
   ___ + ___ = ___
   $7 - 4 = $ ___
   ___ − ___ = ___

Write your own fact families.

3. ___ + ___ = ___
   ___ + ___ = ___
   ___ − ___ = ___
   ___ − ___ = ___

4.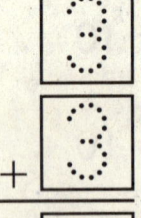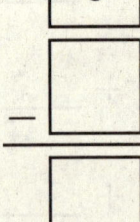

Problem Solving *Number Sense*

Circle all the answers that go with the problem.

5. There are 5 boys at the party.
   There are 6 girls at the party.
   How many children are at the party?
   $5 + 6$ $6 - 5$ 11 children

6. 5 boys left the party.
   Now how many children are at the party?
   $11 + 5$ $11 - 5$ 6 children

Name _____

Finding the Missing Part

P 1-11

Use counters.
Find out how many objects are in the bag.

1. There are 8 balls in all.
   How many balls are in the bag?   4 + __4__ = 8

   __4__ balls are in the bag.

2. There are 9 yo-yos in all.
   How many yo-yos are in the bag?   2 + ____ = 9

   ____ yo-yos are in the bag.

3. There are 10 whistles in all.
   How many whistles are in the bag?   6 + ____ = 10

   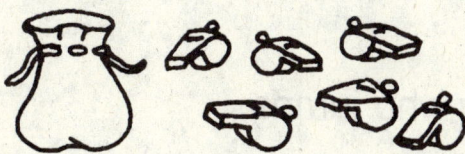

   ____ whistles are in the bag.

Problem Solving *Algebra*

4. Pick 3 numbers from the hat.
   Write an addition and a
   subtraction sentence.

   _____

   _____

Use with Lesson 1-11.

Name _____

PROBLEM-SOLVING APPLICATIONS　　　　　　　　　　　　P 1-12

Frogs and Toads

Solve the problems.

1. A frog eats 3 mealworms. A toad eats 7 mealworms. How many more mealworms does the toad eat?

   7 − 3 = _____ mealworms

2. There are 7 bullfrogs on a rock. 6 more bullfrogs join them. How many bullfrogs in all are on the rock now?

   _____ ◯ _____ ◯ _____ bullfrogs

3. One American toad is 2 inches long. A second American toad is 4 inches long. How long are the two toads together?

   _____ ◯ _____ ◯ _____ inches

Writing in Math

4. Write a number story about a frog who jumps and then jumps again.

   _____

   _____

   _____

5. Stan has 11 tree frogs. Joy has 4 tree frogs. How many more tree frogs does Stan have?

   _____ ◯ _____ ◯ _____ tree frogs

12　Use with Lesson 1-12.

Name _____

Counting On

P 2-1

Count on to find each sum.

1. $11 + 3 = \underline{14}$ $14 + 2 = \underline{}$ $18 + 3 = \underline{}$

2. $2 + 17 = \underline{}$ $\underline{} = 16 + 1$ $\underline{} = 2 + 14$

3. $19 + 2 = \underline{}$ $\underline{} = 11 + 2$ $3 + 19 = \underline{}$

4. $\underline{} = 13 + 2$ $18 + 1 = \underline{}$ $2 + 15 = \underline{}$

5. $13 + 3 = \underline{}$ $2 + 12 = \underline{}$ $\underline{} = 3 + 11$

6. | 15 | 13 | 12 | 18 | 12 | 19 |
    |----|----|----|----|----|----|
    | +3 | +2 | +2 | +3 | +1 | +3 |

7. | 14 | 17 | 13 | 19 | 16 | 12 |
    |----|----|----|----|----|----|
    | +3 | +1 | +2 | +2 | +2 | +3 |

Problem Solving Number Sense

Write a number sentence to solve each story. Solve.

8. Pam bought 13 flowers. Mark bought 3 flowers. How many flowers did they buy in all?

   ____ + ____ = ____ flowers

9. Lee collected 16 rocks. Meg collected 2 rocks. How many rocks did they collect in all?

   ____ + ____ = ____ rocks

Use with Lesson 2-1.

Name _____

Doubles Facts to 18

P 2-2

Solve. Circle the doubles facts.

1. ((12)) = 6 + 6   16 + 2 = ____   ____ = 3 + 14

2. 15 + 1 = ____   ____ = 1 + 1   2 + 18 = ____

3. 7 + 7 = ____   ____ = 13 + 3   8 + 8 = ____

4. 15   9   11   19   2   16
  +3   +9   +2   +1   +2   +3

5. 6   16   1   14   5   18
  +6   +1   +1   +2   +5   +3

6. 3   17   15   8   13   0
  +3   +1   +2   +8   +2   +0

Problem Solving Visual Thinking

Draw a picture to solve the problem.
Write the number sentence.

7. Carissa counted 5 black buttons. Maurice counted the same number of white buttons. How many buttons did they count in all?

____ + ____ = ____

14   Use with Lesson 2-2.

Doubles Plus 1

Add. Use doubles facts to help you.

1.   5   8   9   5   2   4
    + 5   + 9   + 9   + 6   + 2   + 3
    10

2. 10   7   8   0   4   8
    + 9   + 7   + 7   + 0   + 5   + 8

3.   7   6   4   6   3   2
    + 8   + 7   + 4   + 5   + 3   + 3

4. 7 + 6 = _____   5 + 4 = _____   _____ = 3 + 4

5. 9 + 10 = _____   4 + 4 = _____   9 + 8 = _____

Problem Solving *Writing in Math*

6. Use pictures, numbers, or words to tell how 6 + 8 and 6 + 6 are related.

Using Strategies to Add Three Numbers

Add. Try different ways.

1. $3 + 7 + 3 = \underline{13}$

2. $\underline{} = 3 + 6 + 6$

3. $6 + 4 + 5 = \underline{}$

4. $\underline{} = 8 + 0 + 8$

5.
```
  10      9      6      4      4      8
   3      2      5      1      6      3
  +5     +2     +4     +9     +5     +8
```

6.
```
   5      6      8      2      5      9
   8      3      3      8      7      0
  +4     +7     +6     +8     +3     +8
```

Problem Solving *Algebra*

Find the missing numbers. The same shapes are the same numbers.

The numbers in ◯ are sums. Add across and down.

7.
8	△	8	⑱
7	9	△	⑱
□	7	8	⑱
⑱	⑱	⑱	

8.
9	3	2	⑭
⏢	6	⏢	⑭
1	⌂	8	⑭
⑭	⑭	⑭	

△ = ____ □ = ____   ⏢ = ____ ⌂ = ____

Name _____

Making 10 to Add 9

P 2-5

Add. Use counters and Workmat 3 if you need to.

1.   9   6   0   9   2   5
   + 3   + 9   + 9   + 8   + 9   + 9
   ―――   ―――   ―――   ―――   ―――   ―――
    12

2.   9   9   3   9   5   9
   + 7   + 1   + 9   + 8   + 9   + 6

3.   9   4   7   9   9   8
   + 5   + 9   + 9   + 5   + 2   + 9

4. 9 + 7 = ____   6 + 9 = ____   4 + 9 = ____

Problem Solving *Reasoning*

Solve by using pictures, numbers, or words.

5. Shana had 9 pins in her collection. She bought more pins. Now she has 17 pins. How many pins did Shana buy?

Use with Lesson 2-5.   **17**

Name _____

Making 10 to Add 7 or 8

P 2-6

Add. Use counters and Workmat 3 if you need to.

1.   8   5   4   8   7   9
   + 3   + 9   + 7   + 8   + 9   + 5
    11

2.   8   4   6   8   5   7
   + 7   + 8   + 7   + 6   + 7   + 8

3. 4 + 8 = ____   10 + 7 = ____   0 + 8 = ____

4. 7 + 7 = ____   9 + 3 = ____   ____ = 9 + 10

Problem Solving *Algebra*

Find the pattern. Write the missing numbers.

5.   7 + 9 = 10 + 6

    7 + 8 = 10 + ☐

    7 + ☐ = 10 + 4

    7 + ☐ = 10 + ☐

    ☐ + ☐ = ☐ + ☐

Use with Lesson 2-6.

PROBLEM-SOLVING STRATEGY

Write a Number Sentence

Write a number sentence to solve the problem.
Use the table to help you.

Game Scores			
Teams	Game 1	Game 2	Game 3
Robins	7	4	6
Bluejays	5	8	5

1. How many points did the Bluejays score altogether in Games 1 and 2?

    $5 + 8$ = 13 points

2. How many points did the Robins score altogether in Games 1 and 2?

    _____ = _____ points

3. Which team had scored more points after Game 2? _____

4. How many points did the Robins score altogether?

    _____ = _____ points

5. How many points did the Bluejays score altogether?

    _____ = _____ points

6. Which team, the Robins or the Bluejays, scored more points altogether? _____

Name _____

Counting Back

P 2-8

Subtract. Use the number line if you need to.

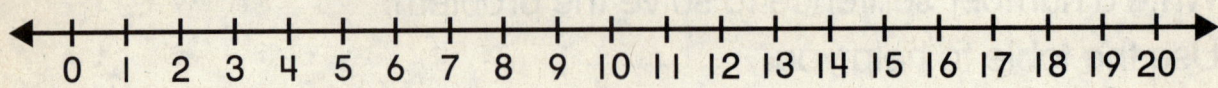

1. $16 - 2 =$ _____ $14 - 3 =$ _____   _____ $= 13 - 1$

2. $15 - 2 =$ _____   _____ $= 12 - 3$ $18 - 2 =$ _____

3.
11	14	19	17	13	12
−3	−2	−1	−3	−2	−2

4.
11	17	13	15	18	16
−2	−2	−3	−3	−1	−3

5.
19	14	15	18	13	19
−3	−1	−2	−3	−2	−1

Problem Solving *Writing in Math*

Write a story or draw a picture
to go with the problem.
Then solve.

6. $16 - 5 =$ _____

Name _____

Thinking Doubles to Subtract

P 2-9

Subtract. Write the doubles fact that helps you.

1. 10 − 5 = ____

    ____ + ____ = ____

    If 5 + 5 = 10 then 10 − 5 = 5

2. 20 − 10 = ____

    ____ + ____ = ____

3. ____ = 12 − 6

    ____ = ____ + ____

4. 6 − 3 = ____

    ____ + ____ = ____

5. ____ = 14 − 7

    ____ = ____ + ____

6.   8
    − 4
    ____
    [ ]

    [ ]
    + [ ]
    ____
    [ ]

7.   18
    − 9
    ____
    [ ]

    [ ]
    + [ ]
    ____
    [ ]

Problem Solving *Writing in Math*

8. Krista and Alan have 12 action figures. How could they share the action figures so they each have an equal amount?

Use with Lesson 2-9. **21**

Thinking Addition to Subtract

P 2-10

Solve. Draw a line to match each subtraction fact with its related addition fact.

1. $14 - 8 = \underline{6}$ $5 + \underline{} = 11$

   $16 - 7 = \underline{}$ $2 + \underline{} = 18$

   $11 - 5 = \underline{}$ $8 + \underline{6} = 14$

   $18 - 2 = \underline{}$ $7 + \underline{} = 16$

2. $\underline{} = 15 - 6$ $13 = 5 + \underline{}$

   $\underline{} = 12 - 7$ $15 = 6 + \underline{}$

   $\underline{} = 17 - 3$ $17 = 3 + \underline{}$

   $\underline{} = 13 - 5$ $12 = 7 + \underline{}$

Problem Solving Mental Math

3. Randy has 20¢. He bought a used toy truck for 14¢. Circle the used toy that he has enough money left to buy.

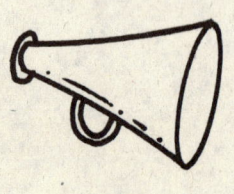
8¢

10¢

5¢

22 Use with Lesson 2-10.

Name _____

PROBLEM-SOLVING SKILL P 2-11

Use Data from a Picture

Find the missing number.
Write the number sentence.

1. What does the cube weigh?

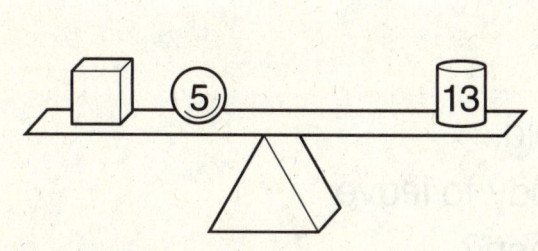

If ___8___ + 5 = 13,

then 13 − 5 = ___8___

The cube weighs ___8___ pounds.

2. What does the cylinder weigh?

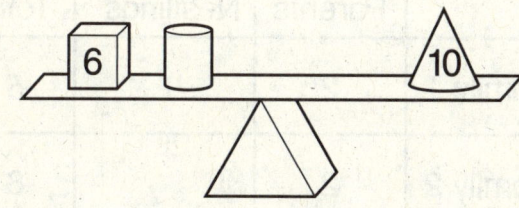

If 6 + ____ = 10,

then 10 − 6 = ____

The cylinder weighs ____ pounds.

Reasoning

Write the missing number for each sentence.

3. ____ + 8 = 17   4. 14 − ____ = 9

   7 + ____ = 13   15 − ____ = 8

Use with Lesson 2-11. **23**

Name _____

PROBLEM-SOLVING APPLICATIONS   P 2-12

Baby Birds

Solve.

1. A nest has 13 eggs, and 5 of the eggs hatch.
   How many more eggs need to hatch?

   _____ – _____ = _____ eggs

2. A group of nestlings is 8 days old.
   In 9 more days, they will be ready to leave
   the nest. How old will they be then?

   _____ ◯ _____ = _____ days old

3. Look at the chart. How
   many nestlings are in
   the second family?

	Parents	Nestlings	Total
Family 1	2	4	6
Family 2	2	_____	8

   2 + _____ = 8

   There are _____ nestlings in the second family.

Writing in Math

4. A group of 3 birds was at the bird feeder.
   Then 12 more birds came and chased them away.
   How many birds were left at the bird feeder?

   _____

24   Use with Lesson 2-12.

Name _____

Counting with Tens and Ones

P 3-1

Circle groups of ten. Count the tens and ones.
Write the numbers.

1.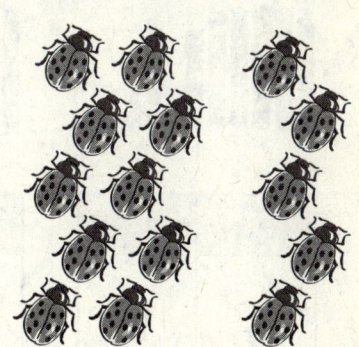

_____ tens and _____ ones is _____ in all.

2.

_____ tens and _____ ones is _____ in all.

Problem Solving *Number Sense*

Solve.

3. Beth has 6 tens and 2 ones. Bobby gives her 1 more one. What is the number?

   _____ tens and _____ ones

   is _____ in all.

4. Luis has 4 tens and 5 ones. Shayla gives him 1 more ten. What is the number?

   _____ tens and _____ ones

   is _____ in all.

Name _____

P 3-2

Using Tens and Ones

Draw lines to match the numbers.
Use cubes and Workmat 4 if you need to.

1.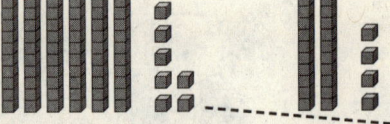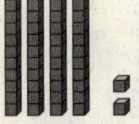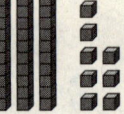

Tens	Ones
4	2

Tens	Ones
3	8

Tens	Ones
2	4

Tens	Ones
6	7

2.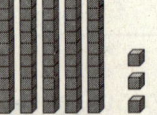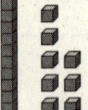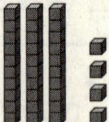

Tens	Ones
1	8

Tens	Ones
5	3

Tens	Ones
4	9

Tens	Ones
3	4

Problem Solving *Visual Thinking*

3. Crayons come in packs of ten.
   How many packs would you need
   to get at least 42 crayons?
   Draw a picture to solve the problem.
   Explain your answer.

   _____ packs

Number Words

P 3-3

Write the number.

1. eight 8   twenty-five ____   forty-nine ____

2. sixty ____   thirteen ____   ninety-two ____

3. fifty-seven ____   eighty-four ____   seventy-three ____

Write the number word.

4. 18 _____   5. 77 _____

6. 5 tens _____   7. 14 ones _____

8. 27 _____   9. 50 _____

10. 1 ten 8 ones _____   11. 3 tens _____

12. 4 tens 8 ones _____

13. 9 tens 2 ones _____

Problem Solving Number Sense

What is the number?

14. It is greater than 30 and less than 40. If you add the digits, the sum is 10. Write the number word.

15. It is greater than 7 tens and less than 8 tens. The number has 4 ones. Write the number word.

Use with Lesson 3-3.

PROBLEM-SOLVING STRATEGY

Make an Organized List

Use only tens to make the number in two parts.
Use cubes and Workmat 1 if you need to.

1. Make 40.

Tens	Tens	Total
0	4	40
		40
		40
		40
		40

2. Make 80.

Tens	Tens	Total
0	8	80
		80
2	6	80
		80
		80
5	3	80
		80
		80
		80

3. Make 70.

Tens	Tens	Total
		70

Comparing Numbers

Write >, <, or =.

1. 32 < 51   15 ◯ 51   43 ◯ 48

2. 70 ◯ 65   48 ◯ 50   93 ◯ 89

3. 27 ◯ 21   67 ◯ 67   70 ◯ 77

4. 19 ◯ 91   82 ◯ 59   12 ◯ 12

Write a number that makes each statement true.

5. ____ > 56   39 = ____   89 > ____

6. ____ < 73   ____ > 35   ____ = 100

Problem Solving *Reasoning*

What number am I?

7. My tens digit is double the ones digit. I am less than 50 and greater than 40.

    ____

8. My ones digit is 5 more than the tens digit. I am greater than 25 and less than 35.

    ____

Use with Lesson 3-5.

Finding the Closest Ten

P 3-6

Find the number on the number line.
Write the closest ten.

1.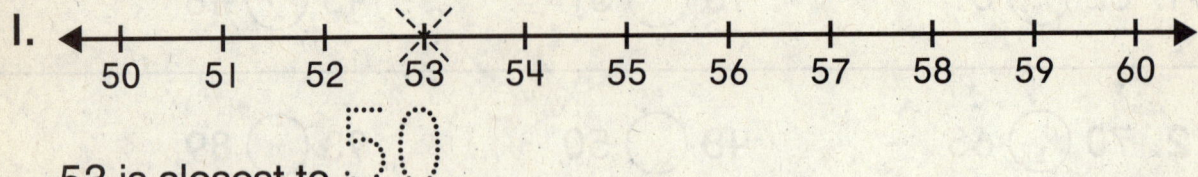

53 is closest to 50.

2.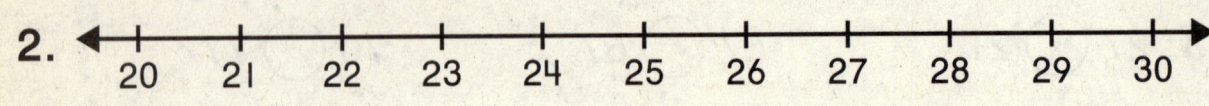

28 is closest to ____.

3.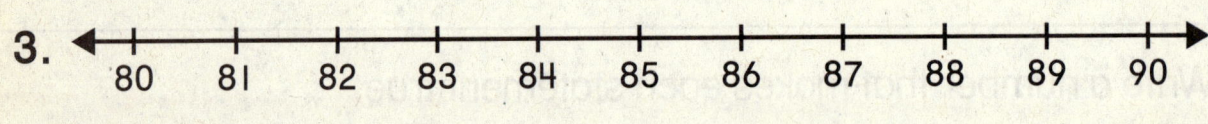

82 is closest to ____.

Write the closest ten.

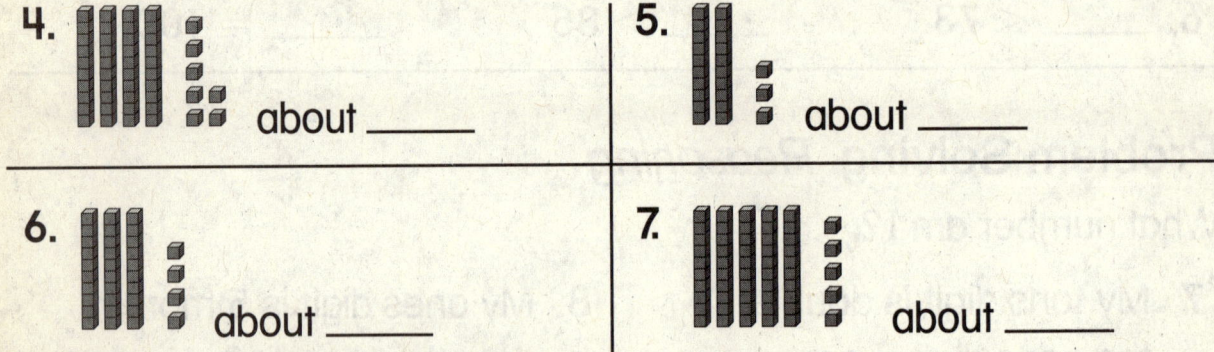

4. about ____

5. about ____

6. about ____

7. about ____

Problem Solving *Reasonableness*

8. Maria has a collection of about 20 toy cars.
Which could be the exact number of cars?

23   32   12   40   ____ toy cars

Before, After, and Between

P 3-7

Write the missing numbers.
Use the hundred chart if you need to.

1	2	3	4	5	6	7	8	9	10
11	12	13	14	15	16	17	18	19	20
21	22	23	24	25	26	27	28	29	30
31	32	33	34	35	36	37	38	39	40
41	42	43	44	45	46	47	48	49	50
51	52	53	54	55	56	57	58	59	60
61	62	63	64	65	66	67	68	69	70
71	72	73	74	75	76	77	78	79	80
81	82	83	84	85	86	87	88	89	90
91	92	93	94	95	96	97	98	99	100

1.

	62	63	
71		73	
		83	85

2.

	71		73
		82	83
	91		

3. _____, 38, _____, _____, 41

4. 49, _____, _____, 52, _____

Write the number.

5. What number is one after 28? _____

6. What number is between 69 and 71? _____

7. What number is one before 45? _____

Problem Solving *Writing in Math*

8. Pick a number from 1 to 100. Describe the number using the words before, after, and between.

Name _____

Skip Counting on the Hundred Chart

P 3-8

1. Finish coloring skip counts by 10s.
2. Circle skip counts by 3s.
3. What patterns do you see with skip counts by 10s and 3s?

_____

_____

1	2	3	4	5	6	7	8	9	10
11	12	13	14	15	16	17	18	19	20
21	22	23	24	25	26	27	28	29	30
31	32	33	34	35	36	37	38	39	40
41	42	43	44	45	46	47	48	49	50
51	52	53	54	55	56	57	58	59	60
61	62	63	64	65	66	67	68	69	70
71	72	73	74	75	76	77	78	79	80
81	82	83	84	85	86	87	88	89	90
91	92	93	94	95	96	97	98	99	100

Problem Solving *Number Sense*

4. Count by 2s.   12, 14, 16, 18, _____, _____, _____, _____

5. Count by 3s.   30, 33, 36, 39, _____, _____, _____, _____

6. Count by 5s.   50, 55, 60, 65, _____, _____, _____, _____

7. Count by 10s. 30, 40, 50, 60, _____, _____, _____, _____

8. Count backward by 2s.   40, 38, 36, 34, _____, _____, _____

9. Count backward by 3s.   30, 27, 24, 21, _____, _____, _____

10. Count backward by 5s.   100, 95, 90, 85, _____, _____, _____

11. Count backward by 10s.   80, 70, 60, 50, _____, _____, _____

Use with Lesson 3-8.

Name _____

Even and Odd Numbers

P 3-9

1. Circle the odd numbers.

2. The ones digit in odd numbers can be _____

(1)	2	(3)	4	5	6	7	8	9	10
11	12	13	14	15	16	17	18	19	20
21	22	23	24	25	26	27	28	29	30
31	32	33	34	35	36	37	38	39	40
41	42	43	44	45	46	47	48	49	50
51	52	53	54	55	56	57	58	59	60

3. The ones digit in even numbers can be _____

Circle the numbers that are odd.

4. 43   44   45   46

Circle the numbers that are even.

5. 19   82   50   71

Write even or odd.

6. 38 _____   67 _____   85 _____

7. 89 _____   22 _____   13 _____

Problem Solving *Algebra*

8. When you add an odd and even number together, is the sum odd or even? Explain. _____

2 + ____ = 5

5 + ____ = 11

Use with Lesson 3-9. **33**

Name _____

Ordinal Numbers Through Twentieth

P 3-10

Use the crayons to solve.
Write the letter or number.

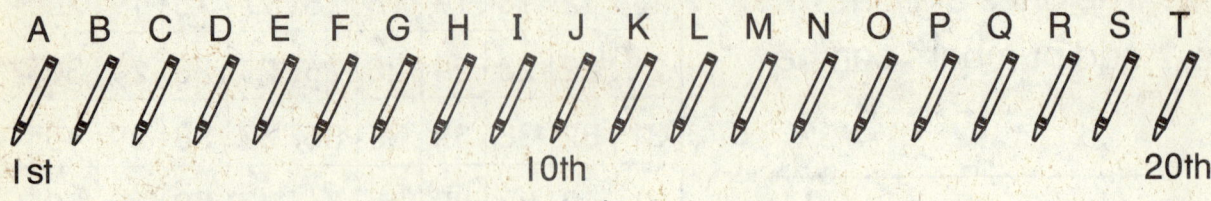

1. The eighth crayon is ___. 2. The 4th crayon is ___.

3. The fifth crayon is ___. 4. The twelfth crayon is ___.

5. How many crayons are before the 16th crayon? ___
6. How many crayons are after the 18th crayon? ___

Mark your answers on the stars.

7. Write an X on the 12th star. 8. Circle the fifteenth star.

9. Write a ✓ on the 20th star. 10. Put a box around the seventh star.

Problem Solving *Reasonableness*

Solve the riddle.

11. This letter comes after the second letter. It comes before the fifth letter. The letter is not a vowel.

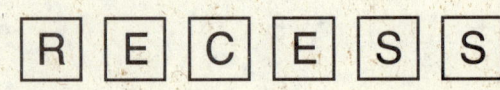

What is the secret letter? ___

34 Use with Lesson 3-10.

Name _____

PROBLEM-SOLVING SKILL　　　　　　　　　　　　P 3-11

Use Data From a Chart

Use clues to find the secret number.
Cross out the numbers on the chart
that do not fit the clue.

1. It is greater than 47.
   It has a 4 in the tens place.
   It is an even number.

30	31	32	33	34	35	36	37	38	39
40	41	42	43	44	45	46	47	48	49
50	51	52	53	54	55	56	57	58	59

   The secret number is _____.

2. It is less than 64.
   It has 5 ones.

50	51	52	53	54	55	56	57	58	59
60	61	62	63	64	65	66	67	68	69
70	71	72	73	74	75	76	77	78	79

   The secret number is _____.

3. It has 8 tens.
   It is greater than 87.
   It is an odd number.

70	71	72	73	74	75	76	77	78	79
80	81	82	83	84	85	86	87	88	89
90	91	92	93	94	95	96	97	98	99

   The secret number is _____.

Problem Solving *Writing in Math*

4. Choose an odd number
   between 31 and 59.
   Write 3 clues. Ask a friend
   to find your secret number.

Clues: _____

_____

_____

_____

Use with Lesson 3-11.

Name _____

Dime, Nickel, and Penny

P 3-12

Count on to find the total amount.

1.

   10¢ ____ ____ ____ ____

Total Amount

2.

   ____ ____ ____ ____ ____

Total Amount

3.

   ____ ____ ____ ____ ____

Total Amount

4.

   ____ ____ ____ ____ ____

Total Amount

Problem Solving *Writing in Math*

5. Which stack of money would you like to spend? Explain.

_____

_____

Use with Lesson 3-12.

Name _____

Quarter and Half-Dollar

P 3-13

Count on to find the total amount.
You may use Workmat 6 if you need to.

1.

   25¢ _____ _____ _____ _____

Total Amount

2.

   _____ _____ _____ _____ _____

Total Amount

3.

   _____ _____ _____ _____ _____

Total Amount

Problem Solving *Number Sense*

4. Pam has 4 coins in her pocket.
   The coins total 50¢.
   Color the coins Pam has.

Use with Lesson 3-13. **37**

Name _____

Counting Sets of Coins

P 3-14

Draw coins from the greatest to the least value.
Count on to find the total amount.

1.

   25¢ ___ ___ ___ ___

   The total amount is _____.

2.

   ___ ___ ___ ___

   The total amount is _____.

3.

   ___ ___ ___ ___ ___

   The total amount is _____.

Problem Solving *Estimation*

4. Kobe has about 50¢. Circle the coins he might have.

38 Use with Lesson 3-14.

Comparing Sets of Coins

P 3-15

Write the total amounts and compare them.
Write >, <, or =.

1.

   _65¢_ ◯ _____

2.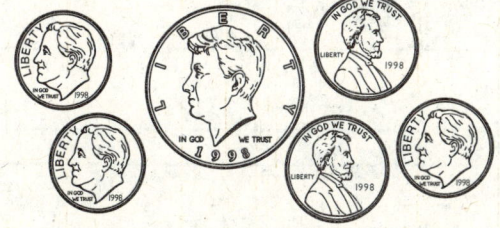

   _____ ◯ _____

3.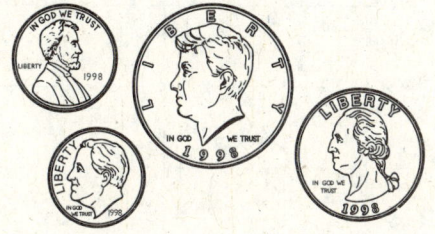

   _____ ◯ _____

Problem Solving *Reasoning*

4. Draw coins that have a value of more than 42¢ but less than 95¢.

Use with Lesson 3-15. **39**

Name _____

Ways to Show the Same Amount

P 3-16

Use coins to show the same amount in different ways. Record with tally marks.

Ways to Show 80¢

Half Dollar	Dime	Nickel	Total Amount
1.			
2.			
3.			
4.			
5.			

Which row shows the fewest number of coins used?

_____

Ways to Show 66¢

Quarter	Dime	Penny	Total Amount
6.			
7.			
8.			
9.			

Which row shows the fewest number of coins used?

_____

Problem Solving Reasoning

10. Jamal has coins in a piggy bank. Circle the coin Jamal needs to put in the bank to make 75¢.

40 Use with Lesson 3-16.

Name _____

Making Change

P 3-17

Count on from the price.
Draw the coins you would get for change.
Write the amount of change.

Price	You Give	You Get	Change
1. apple 12¢	15¢	(12¢) 13¢ 14¢ 15¢	3¢
2. pear 23¢	30¢	(23¢) ___ ___ ___	___
3. pineapple 74¢	90¢	(74¢) ___ ___ ___	___
4. watermelon 89¢	$1.00	(89¢) ___ ___ ___	___

Problem Solving *Algebra*

5. Michael has 34¢.
   He needs 45¢ to buy a toy.
   Circle the coins Michael needs.
   Write the number.

34¢ + _____ = 45¢

Name _____

Dollar Bill and Dollar Coin

P 3-18

Write each total amount.
Circle sets of coins that equal one dollar.

1.

Total Amount
80¢

2.

Total Amount

3.

Total Amount

4.

Total Amount

Problem Solving *Algebra*

5. Draw the coin that makes each set the same amount.

   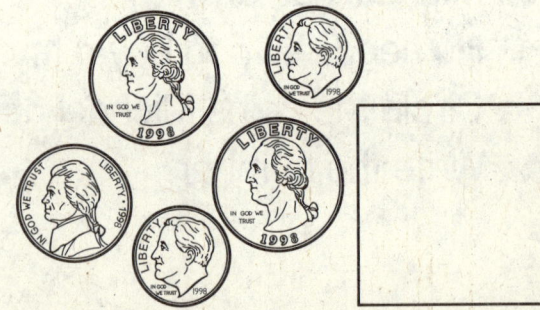

42 Use with Lesson 3-18.

Name _____

PROBLEM-SOLVING APPLICATIONS P 3-19

Money, Money, Money

Solve.

1. Count on to find how much in all.

$10.00   _____   _____   _____

2. Rob collects buffalo nickels.
   Each page in the book holds 5 nickels.
   How many nickels will fill 5 pages?
   Draw the nickels on the pages.

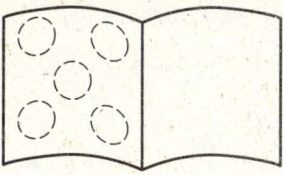 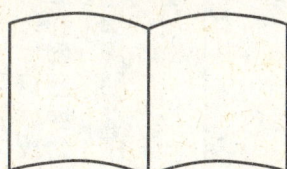 

____ ____ ____ ____ ____ nickels in all.

Writing in Math

3. Every year, 5 states get their own quarter.
   Each state quarter has a different picture on it.
   Tell what picture you would draw for your
   state's quarter. Draw your quarter.

   _____

   _____

Name _____

Adding Tens

P 4-1

Add tens. Use mental math or cubes.

1.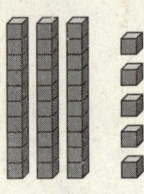
   35 + 20 = 55

2.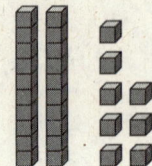
   ____ + 40 = ____

3.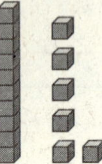
   ____ + 40 = ____

4.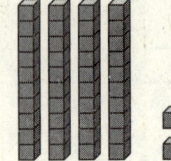
   ____ + 10 = ____

5.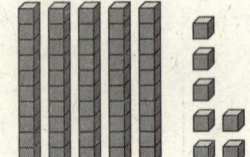
   ____ + 30 = ____

6.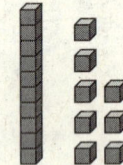
   ____ + 20 = ____

7.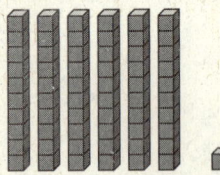
   ____ + 10 = ____

8.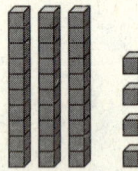
   ____ + 30 = ____

Problem Solving Number Sense

9. Allie had 38¢. On Thursday she found 10¢, and on Friday she found 10¢ more. How much money does she have now? ____¢

Use with Lesson 4-1.

Name _____

Adding Ones

P 4-2

Add ones. Use mental math or cubes.

1.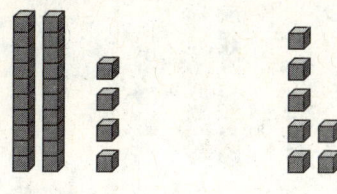

    24 + 7 = 31

2.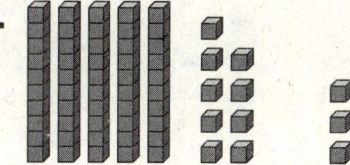

    59 + 3 = ____

3.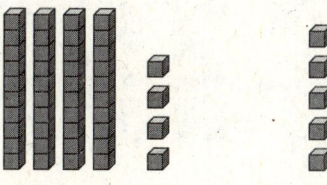

    44 + 5 = ____

4.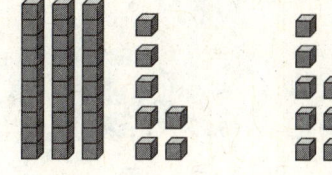

    37 + 8 = ____

5.

    17 + 6 = ____

6.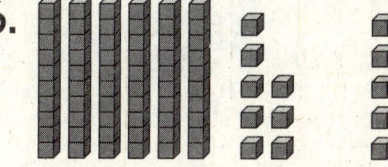

    68 + 5 = ____

Problem Solving *Algebra*

Circle the weights that answer the question.

7. What weights can you put on the scale to make it balance?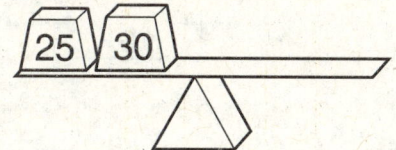

Name _____

Adding Tens and Ones

P 4-3

Add. Use mental math or cubes.

1. 62 and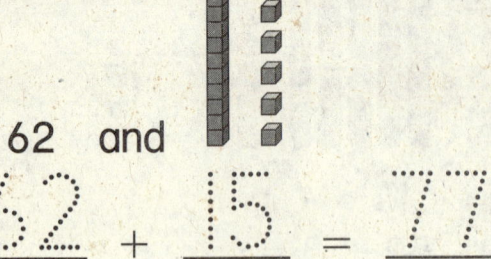

   $\underline{62} + \underline{15} = \underline{77}$

2. 35 and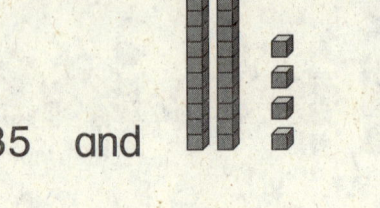

   ___ + ___ = ___

3. 41 and

   ___ + ___ = ___

4. 13 and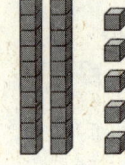

   ___ + ___ = ___

5. 26 and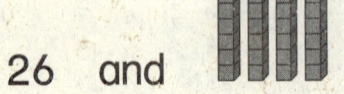

   ___ + ___ = ___

6. 57 and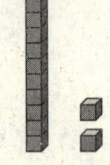

   ___ + ___ = ___

7. 32 and

   ___ + ___ = ___

8. 45 and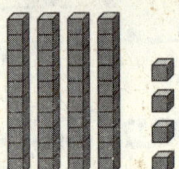

   ___ + ___ = ___

Problem Solving *Number Sense*

Circle the ones digit to make the number sentence true.

9. 35 + 2▢ = 59

       3   4   5

10. 4▢ + 36 = 78

        2   4   6

Use with Lesson 4-3.

Name _____

Estimating Sums

P 4-4

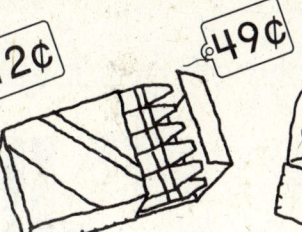
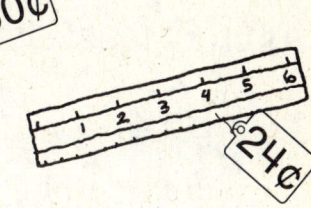

Estimate. Circle **yes** or **no** to answer the question for each exercise.

You have	Can you buy these items?	Answer
1. 50¢	notebook and pencil	(yes) / no
2. 70¢	ruler and crayons	yes / no
3. 60¢	pencil and pencil sharpener	yes / no
4. 80¢	notebook and crayons	yes / no

Problem Solving *Reasoning*

5. Sam has 45¢. He has exactly enough money to buy both toys. How much does the car cost? _____

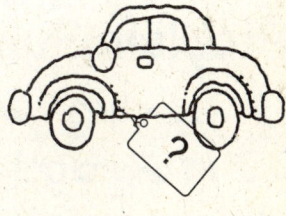

Use with Lesson 4-4.

Name _____

P 4-5

Subtracting Tens

Subtract tens. Use mental math or cubes.

1.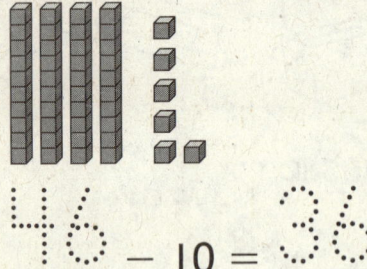
   46 − 10 = 36

2.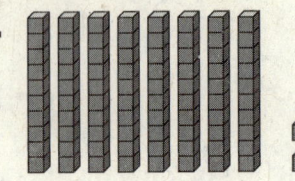
   ___ − 30 = ___

3.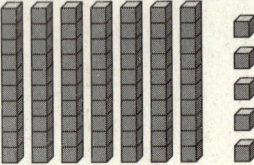
   ___ − 40 = ___

4.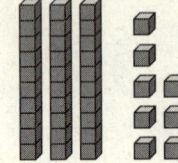
   ___ − 20 = ___

5.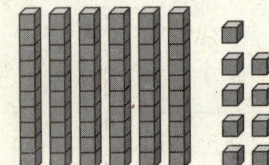
   ___ − 40 = ___

6.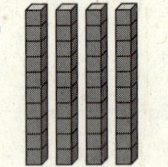
   ___ − 10 = ___

7.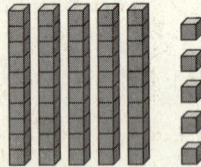
   ___ − 30 = ___

8.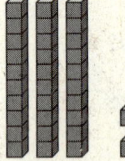
   ___ − 20 = ___

Problem Solving *Mental Math*

9. Nick has 90¢. He used his money to buy a bat and a ball. How much money does he have left? ___ ¢

Use with Lesson 4-5.

Subtracting Tens and Ones

P 4-6

Subtract. Use mental math or cubes.

1.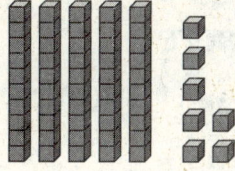
57 − 14 = __43__

2.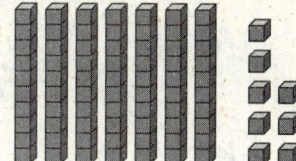
78 − 25 = _____

3.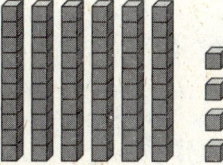
64 − 22 = _____

4.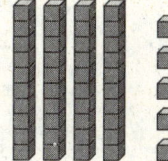
45 − 32 = _____

5.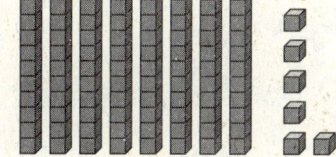
86 − 21 = _____

6.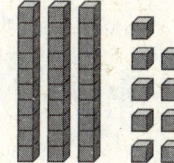
39 − 13 = _____

7.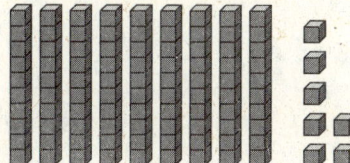
97 − 46 = _____

8.
73 − 41 = _____

Problem Solving *Writing in Math*

9. Draw cubes to show 56 − 23.
   Describe how you found the difference.

Use with Lesson 4-6.

Name _____

Estimating Differences

P 4-7

Estimate. Circle **more** or **less** to complete each sentence.

1. 70 − 33 is (less) / more than 40.

2. 90 − 42 is more / less than 50.

3. 50 − 24 is more / less than 30.

4. 80 − 17 is more / less than 60.

5. 30 − 15 is more / less than 10.

6. 40 − 21 is more / less than 20.

7. 60 − 13 is more / less than 50.

8. 70 − 49 is more / less than 20.

Problem Solving *Reasonableness*

Circle the more reasonable estimate.

9. There is room for 60 people on the bus. 27 people are already on the bus. About how many people can still fit on the bus?

   20 people
   30 people
   40 people

10. There were 40 people at the movie. 18 people left. About how many people are still at the movie?

    10 people
    20 people
    30 people

50 Use with Lesson 4-7.

Name _____

PROBLEM-SOLVING STRATEGY   P 4-8

Try, Check, and Revise

Find pairs of numbers with the given sum.
The sum of the ones digits must be 10.

1. | 52 | 24 | 18 | 46 |

    Numbers with a sum of 70

    _52_ and _18_

    ____ and ____

2. | 18 | 39 | 11 | 32 |

    Numbers with a sum of 50

    ____ and ____

    ____ and ____

3. | 23 | 57 | 48 | 32 |

    Numbers with a sum of 80

    ____ and ____

    ____ and ____

4. | 45 | 33 | 15 | 27 |

    Numbers with a sum of 60

    ____ and ____

    ____ and ____

Name _____

Addition and Subtraction Patterns

P 4-9

What is the pattern? Write the numbers.

1. 20, 25, 30, 35, 40, __45__, _____, _____, _____,

   _____, _____, _____, _____, _____, _____, _____

   What is the pattern? _____

2. 69, 66, 63, 60, _____, _____, _____, _____, _____, _____,

   _____, _____, _____, _____, _____, _____, _____, _____

   What is the pattern? _____

Problem Solving *Algebra*

Find the pattern. Write the missing numbers.

3. 30 and 4 is 34.

   40 and 4 is _____.

   50 and _____ is _____.

   _____ and _____ is _____.

   _____ and _____ is _____.

4. 58 take away 5 is 53.

   48 take away 5 is _____.

   38 take away _____ is _____.

   _____ take away _____ is _____.

   _____ take away _____ is _____.

Name _____

Finding Parts of 100

P 4-10

Add on to find the other part of 100.
Use mental math or cubes.

1. 40 and __60__ is 100.

2. 65 and _____ is 100.

3. 20 and _____ is 100.

4. 95 and _____ is 100.

5. 45 and _____ is 100.

6. 70 and _____ is 100.

7. 50 and _____ is 100.

8. 90 and _____ is 100.

9. 15 and _____ is 100.

10. 75 and _____ is 100.

11. 5 and _____ is 100.

12. 10 and _____ is 100.

13. 30 and _____ is 100.

14. 35 and _____ is 100.

Problem Solving *Algebra*

15. If 60 and __40__ is 100,

    then 100 take away 60 is __40__.

16. If 45 and _____ is 100,

    then 100 take away 45 is _____.

Use with Lesson 4-10. **53**

Name _____

PROBLEM-SOLVING SKILL   P 4-11

Look Back and Check

Circle the number that makes sense.

1. Vinnie has 30 baseball cards.
   His friend gave him 15 more cards.
   Now Vinnie has 45 / 15 baseball cards.

2. Mary painted 11 pictures.
   Simon painted 8 pictures.
   Together, Mary and Simon painted 3 / 19 pictures.

3. Scott collected 42 coins.
   He put 12 coins in an album.
   There are 30 / 54 coins out of the album.

4. Debbie made 52 puppets for the craft fair.
   She sold 22 of the puppets.
   Now Debbie has 30 / 54 puppets left.

Problem Solving *Visual Thinking*

5. How many cubes are there in all? Circle your answer.

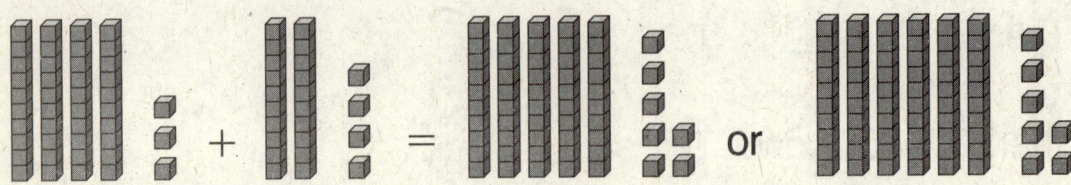

Name _____

PROBLEM-SOLVING APPLICATION   P 4-12

Take Me Out to the Ball Game!

Fun Fact!
In 1998, Mark McGwire hit 70 home runs.
In 2001, Barry Bonds hit 73 home runs.

1. How many more home runs did Barry Bonds hit than Mark McGwire?

   ____ − ____ = ____

2. In 1999, McGwire hit 65 home runs. Write the missing numbers.

   65, ____, ____, 68, ____, 70

3. In his last two seasons, McGwire hit 32 and 29 home runs. How many home runs did he hit in all? Is this more or less than the number of home runs he hit in 1998?

   ____ + ____ = ____   _____

Writing in Math

4. There are 9 positions on a baseball field where players stand. Choose a position that you would like to play. Tell why you chose that position.

   _____

   _____

Use with Lesson 4-12.

Name _____

Adding With and Without Regrouping

P 5-1

Use cubes and Workmat 4.
Add. Regroup if you need to.

Show	Add	Do you need to regroup?	Find the sum
1. 24	7	yes	24 + 7 = 31
2. 56	9	_____	56 + 9 = _____
3. 92	6	_____	92 + 6 = _____
4. 35	8	_____	35 + 8 = _____
5. 69	3	_____	69 + 3 = _____
6. 48	5	_____	48 + 5 = _____
7. 70	4	_____	70 + 4 = _____

Problem Solving *Writing in Math*

8. Write 3 different ones numbers you could add to 15 without needing to regroup.

_____

9. Write 3 different ones numbers you could add to 15 where you need to regroup to find the sum.

_____

Use with Lesson 5-1.

Recording Addition

P 5-2

Use cubes and Workmat 4 if needed.
Add. Regroup if you need to.

1.
Tens	Ones
[1]	
3	8
+	5
4	3

Tens	Ones
☐	
6	4
+	9

Tens	Ones
☐	
8	2
+	5

Tens	Ones
☐	
1	9
+	7

2.
Tens	Ones
☐	
2	5
+	7

Tens	Ones
☐	
4	3
+	8

Tens	Ones
☐	
5	6
+	7

Tens	Ones
☐	
9	2
+	4

Problem Solving *Number Sense*

Use the numbers shown. Make the sum of the numbers across equal the sum of the numbers down.

3.   7 5 1 9 3

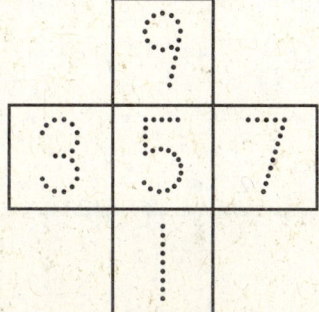

4.   4 7 8 6 5

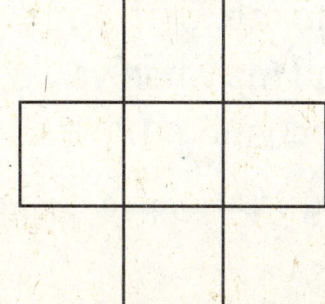

Use with Lesson 5-2. **57**

Name _____

Adding Two-Digit Numbers With and Without Regrouping

P 5-3

Add. Regroup if you need to.
Use cubes and Workmat 4 if needed.

1.
Tens	Ones
1	
4	3
+1	8
6	1

Tens	Ones
□	
1	8
+3	9

Tens	Ones
□	
5	2
+2	8

Tens	Ones
□	
2	3
+5	2

2.
Tens	Ones
□	
2	4
+1	8

Tens	Ones
□	
2	7
+2	6

Tens	Ones
□	
1	3
+7	5

Tens	Ones
□	
8	0
+1	7

Problem Solving *Reasonableness*

Use the number clues to solve.

3. I am a number between 24 and 34.
   You get to me when you count by twos.
   You get to me when you count by fives.
   What number am I?

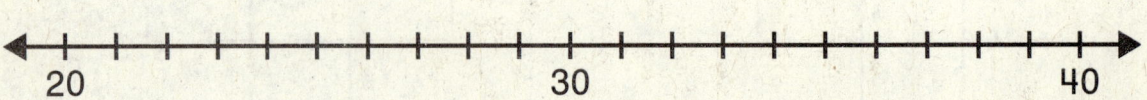

I am the number _____.

Name _____

Practice with Two-Digit Addition

P 5-4

Write the addition problem. Find the sum.

1. 34 + 29   15 + 34   25 + 48   36 + 30

Tens	Ones
1	
3	4
+2	9
6	3

Tens	Ones
+	

Tens	Ones
+	

Tens	Ones
+	

2. 56 + 29   45 + 25   36 + 17   34 + 57

Tens	Ones
+	

Tens	Ones
+	

Tens	Ones
+	

Tens	Ones
+	

Problem Solving *Algebra*

3. Write the missing number in each box. You will need to regroup when you add.

```
  4 5        3 2
+ 2 ☐      + 1 ☐
-----      -----
  7 2        5 1
```

Use with Lesson 5-4. **59**

Name _____

Adding Money

P 5-5

Add to find the total amount.

1.
   1
  1 7¢
+ 4 5¢
———
  6 2¢

   2 4¢
+ 1 9¢

   6 8¢
+ 2 2¢

   4 4¢
+ 1 5¢

2.
   5 2¢
+ 2 7¢

   1 4¢
+ 6 9¢

   2 8¢
+ 1 9¢

   6 2¢
+ 2 6¢

3.
   4 5¢
+ 2 6¢

   2 5¢
+ 3 1¢

   1 7¢
+ 4 4¢

   6 1¢
+ 2 9¢

Problem Solving *Visual Thinking*

4. Jessie has 35¢. He wants to spend all of his money. Which 2 pieces of fruit can he buy? Circle them.

Use with Lesson 5-5.

Adding Three Numbers

P 5-6

Add in any order.

1.
```
  45        16        23        36
  15        25        37        14
+ 26      +  6      + 12      + 26
----      ----      ----      ----
  86
```

2.
```
  31        28        37        28
   8        25        12        47
+ 44      + 41      + 18      + 13
----      ----      ----      ----
```

3.
```
  29        34        52        43
  11         7        15        21
+ 22      + 16      + 26      + 13
----      ----      ----      ----
```

Problem Solving *Reasoning*

    6

4. Use the numbers on the cards to write 2 two-digit numbers that have the sum of 78.

5. Use the numbers on the cards to write 2 two-digit numbers that have the sum of 83.

Use with Lesson 5-6. **61**

PROBLEM-SOLVING SKILL

Use Data from a Table

Use the data from the table to solve the problems.

Sports Books in the Library					
Kind	Baseball	Football	Soccer	Hockey	Tennis
Number	47	36	25	33	8

1. How many books about football and soccer are there in all?

   _61_ books

   $$\begin{array}{r} 36 \\ +25 \\ \hline 61 \end{array}$$

2. How many books about baseball and hockey are there in all?

   _____ books

3. How many books about football, soccer, and tennis are there in all?

   _____ books

4. If the library got 18 more books about baseball, how many baseball books would there be?

   _____ books

Estimating Sums

P 5-8

Estimate the sum. Then solve and compare.

Find the closest 10	Estimate	Solve
1. 53 + 28 53 is closest to _____. 28 is closest to _____.	53 + 28 is about _____.	53 + 28 = _____
2. 36 + 23 36 is closest to _____. 23 is closest to _____.	36 + 23 is about _____.	36 + 23 = _____
3. 67 + 18 67 is closest to _____. 18 is closest to _____.	67 + 18 is about _____.	67 + 18 = _____

Problem Solving *Estimation*

Circle the best estimate.

4. Brittany has 27 animal stickers. Her brother has 33 animal stickers. About how many stickers do they have in all?

   about 50 stickers

   about 60 stickers

   about 70 stickers

Use with Lesson 5-8.

Ways to Add

P 5-9

Write the way you will solve the problem.
Then add and write the sum.

- mental math
- paper and pencil
- cubes
- calculator

1. 28 + 22 = __50__
   mental math,
   paper and pencil

2. 48 + 29 = ____

3. 53 + 7 = ____

4. 36 + 19 = ____

5. 60 + 28 = ____

6. 45 + 25 = ____

Problem Solving *Mental Math*

7. Lisa bought some fruit. She spent 87¢. Which two pieces of fruit did she buy? Circle them.

64 Use with Lesson 5-9.

Name _____

PROBLEM-SOLVING STRATEGY

P 5-10

Try, Check, and Revise

Children bought flowers for school. What did they buy? Try and check to solve each problem.

Flower Prices	
Flower	Price
Rose	52¢
Daisy	25¢
Tulip	37¢
Pansy	23¢
Violet	48¢

1. Tammy paid 71¢ for 2 flowers. What did she buy?

   ___pansy___ and ___violet___

2. Rico paid 89¢ for 2 flowers. What did he buy?

   _____ and _____

3. Katie paid 48¢ for 2 flowers. What did she buy?

   _____ and _____

4. Glen paid 85¢ for 3 flowers. What did he buy?

   _____, _____, and _____

Problem Solving *Algebra*

5. Zack spent 55¢ for two flowers. One flower cost 30¢. Circle the coin that shows how much Zack spent on the other flower.

Use with Lesson 5-10. **65**

Name _____

PROBLEM-SOLVING APPLICATIONS P 5-11

The Wonderful World of Plants

Fun Fact!
Some meat-eating plants trap animals such as worms, or even tiny frogs.

Solve.

1. One group of plants traps 17 insects.
   Another group of plants traps 28 insects.
   How many insects in all have been trapped?

   __17__ ⊕ __28__ = __45__ insects

2. A plant has 12 traps. Another plant has 13 traps.
   How many traps do the two plants have in all?

   _____ ◯ _____ = _____ traps

3. If one plant can capture one insect in one second,
   how many insects could 25 plants trap in 2 seconds?

   _____ ◯ _____ = _____ insects

Writing in Math

4. Write an addition number story about meat-eating plants.
   Try to use two-digit numbers in your problem.

   _____

   _____

   _____

Subtracting With and Without Regrouping

P 6-1

Put cubes on Workmat 4.
Subtract. Regroup if you need to.

Show	Subtract	Do you need to regroup?	Find the difference.
1. 47	9	yes	47 − 9 = 38
2. 52	6		52 − 6 =
3. 38	5		38 − 5 =
4. 73	8		73 − 8 =
5. 64	7		64 − 7 =
6. 48	5		48 − 5 =
7. 27	4		27 − 4 =

Problem Solving *Visual Thinking*

8. The path is 30 inches long. How much farther does the worm need to crawl to get to the end?

   Pokey crawled 14 inches. He needs to crawl _____ inches farther.

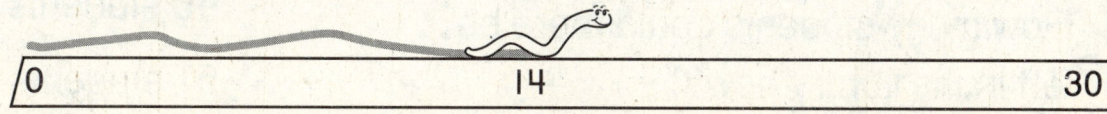

Use with Lesson 6-1.

Recording Subtraction

P 6-2

Subtract. Regroup if you need to.
Use cubes and Workmat 4 if you need to.

1.
Tens	Ones
1̶ (2)	1̶6̶ (6)
	8
1	8

Tens	Ones
5	2
	9

Tens	Ones
7	7
	5

Tens	Ones
3	9
	6

2.
Tens	Ones
4	5
	7

Tens	Ones
6	1
	7

Tens	Ones
5	2
	5

Tens	Ones
9	0
	4

3.
Tens	Ones
7	6
	2

Tens	Ones
3	8
	3

Tens	Ones
6	3
	5

Tens	Ones
2	8
	9

Problem Solving *Reasonableness*

4. There are 45 students in the library. Some of the students leave. How many students could there be left in the library now?

37 students

45 students

51 students

68 Use with Lesson 6-2.

Subtracting Two-Digit Numbers With and Without Regrouping

P 6-3

Subtract. Regroup if you need to.

1.
Tens	Ones
4	13
5̶	3̶
−1	7
3	6

Tens	Ones
6	8
−2	1

Tens	Ones
7	2
−3	8

Tens	Ones
5	3
−4	4

2.
Tens	Ones
8	0
−1	5

Tens	Ones
9	2
−3	6

Tens	Ones
4	8
−2	5

Tens	Ones
2	9
−1	7

3.
Tens	Ones
3	8
−1	9

Tens	Ones
6	1
−2	7

Tens	Ones
8	5
−4	6

Tens	Ones
7	5
−4	7

Problem Solving *Mental Math*

Write the number that makes each number sentence true.

4. 90 − 30 = 80 − ____

   80 − 70 = 20 − ____

5. 70 − 40 = 60 − ____

   60 − 10 = 90 − ____

Use with Lesson 6-3.

Name _____

Practice with Two-Digit Subtraction

P 6-4

Write the subtraction problem. Find the difference.

1.
64 − 39
Tens	Ones
☐	☐
6	4
− 3	9
2	5

45 − 16
Tens	Ones
☐	☐
4	5
− 1	6

72 − 31
Tens	Ones
☐	☐
7	2
− 3	1

56 − 29
Tens	Ones
☐	☐
5	6
− 2	9

2.
84 − 29
Tens	Ones
☐	☐
8	4
− 2	9

34 − 15
Tens	Ones
☐	☐
3	4
− 1	5

96 − 48
Tens	Ones
☐	☐
9	6
− 4	8

43 − 27
Tens	Ones
☐	☐
4	3
− 2	7

Problem Solving *Number Sense*

For each problem, use each number only once. | 1 2 4 5 |

3. Make the greatest sum.

Tens	Ones
☐	☐
+	

4. Make the greatest difference.

Tens	Ones
☐	☐
−	

Name _____

PROBLEM-SOLVING STRATEGY P 6-5

Write a Number Sentence

Write a number sentence to solve the problem.

1. Mel's pet store has 52 birds.
   24 of the birds are parrots.
   How many birds are not parrots?

   52 ⊖ 24 ⊜ 28 birds

   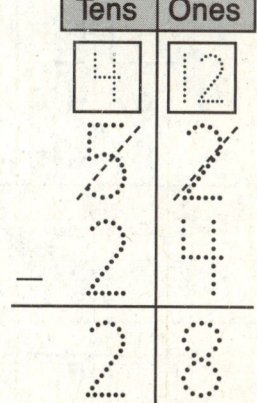

2. Mel orders 47 bags of cat food
   and 38 bags of dog food.
   How many bags does he order in all?

   ___ ◯ ___ ◯ ___ bags

3. There are 78 containers of fish food.
   39 containers of food are sold.
   How many containers are left?

   ___ ◯ ___ ◯ ___ containers

4. The store has 59 dog toys and
   34 cat toys. How many more
   dog toys are there than cat toys?

   ___ ◯ ___ ◯ ___ more dog toys

Use with Lesson 6-5.

Subtracting Money

P 6-6

Subtract to find the difference.

1.
	6	8¢		5	4¢		8	6¢		7	0¢
−	2	3¢	−	1	5¢	−	2	8¢	−	1	6¢
	4	5¢									

2.
	4	3¢		2	4¢		4	9¢		8	3¢
−	2	7¢	−		5¢	−	1	8¢	−	1	8¢

3.
	7	2¢		5	7¢		6	8¢		3	6¢
−	6	3¢	−	1	9¢	−	3	1¢	−	1	9¢

Problem Solving *Reasoning*

Solve. Show your work.

4. Mark has 33¢. He gives 8¢ to his sister. How much money does Mark have left? _____ ¢

5. Jamal has 54¢. He wants to buy a toy that costs 70¢. How much more money does he need? _____ ¢

Use with Lesson 6-6.

Using Addition to Check Subtraction

P 6-7

Subtract. Check your answer by adding.

1.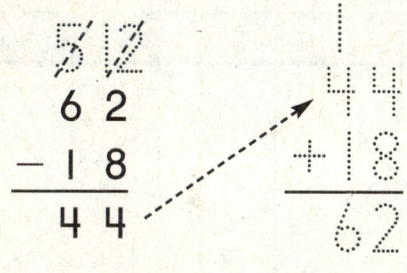

2.
```
  8 3
- 2 9
-----
```

3.
```
  7 3
- 3 7
-----
```

4.
```
  4 8
- 2 1
-----
```

5.
```
  9 4
- 2 8
-----
```

6.
```
  7 5
- 1 7
-----
```

Problem Solving *Algebra*

Write the number that makes each number sentence true.

7. 80 + 10 = 90 – ____

    10 + 30 = 70 – ____

    70 + 10 = 90 – ____

8. 60 – 20 = 20 + ____

    50 – 40 = 10 + ____

    70 – 20 = 10 + ____

Use with Lesson 6-7. **73**

Estimating Differences

P 6-8

Estimate the difference. Then solve and compare.

Find the closest 10	Estimate	Solve
1. 82 − 36 82 is closest to 80. 36 is closest to 40.	80 − 40 ——— 40 82 − 36 is about 40.	82 − 36 = _____
2. 51 − 19 51 is closest to _____. 19 is closest to _____.	51 − 19 is about _____.	51 − 19 = _____
3. 76 − 37 76 is closest to _____. 37 is closest to _____.	76 − 37 is about _____.	76 − 37 = _____

Problem Solving *Estimation*

Circle the best estimate.

4. Andrew has 68 stickers. He gives 32 stickers to his brother. About how many stickers does Andrew have left?

about 30 stickers

about 40 stickers

about 50 stickers

Ways to Subtract

P 6-9

Write the letter that tells how you will solve the problem. Then subtract and write the difference.

| a. mental math | b. cubes |
| c. paper and pencil | d. calculator |

1. b, c, or d

    $5\,10$
    $\cancel{6}\,\cancel{0}$
    $-\;3\,5$
    $\overline{2\,5}$

2. $6\,2$
    $-\;9$
    $\overline{}$

3. $4\,9$
    $-\;7$
    $\overline{}$

4. $8\,3$
    $-\;3\,7$
    $\overline{}$

5. $5\,3$
    $-\;2\,0$
    $\overline{}$

6. $7\,5$
    $-\;2\,6$
    $\overline{}$

7. $4\,6$
    $-\;1\,8$
    $\overline{}$

8. $5\,7$
    $-\;3\,1$
    $\overline{}$

Problem Solving *Writing in Math*

9. Write 2 new subtraction problems that you would use pencil and paper to solve.

Use with Lesson 6-9.

PROBLEM-SOLVING SKILL
Extra Information

Cross out the extra information. Then solve the problem.

1. 45 people ride on the Ferris wheel.
   The Ferris wheel is 38 feet tall.
   63 people ride the bumper cars.
   How many more people ride the bumper cars than the Ferris wheel?

   _____ more people

2. 26 boys and 32 girls ride the water slide.
   41 adults watch the water slide.
   How many children in all ride the water slide?

   _____ children

3. 72 children are waiting to ride the roller coaster. 48 of them get on the next ride. The roller coaster has 24 cars.
   How many children did not get on the ride?

   _____ children

4. A man sells 53 hot dogs and 87 hamburgers.
   He also sells 45 pretzels.
   How many more hamburgers than hot dogs are sold?

   _____ more hamburgers

Use with Lesson 6-10.

PROBLEM-SOLVING APPLICATION P 6-11

Here Kitty, Kitty!

Fun Fact
The cheetah is the fastest animal on land.
It can run up to 70 miles per hour.

1. A cheetah runs at a speed of 70 miles per hour.
   A bus has a speed of 35 miles per hour on a street.
   How much faster is the cheetah's speed than the bus's speed?

   _____ ◯ _____ = _____ miles per hour faster

2. There are 22 lions that live in a pride.
   13 of the lions are cubs.
   How many of the lions are not cubs?

   _____ lions are not cubs.

3. Estimate how much longer the lion is.

   82 is closest to _____.

   68 is closest to _____.

Animal	Length
Lion	About 82 inches
Cheetah	About 68 inches

   So a good estimate of the difference

   would be _____ inches.

Writing in Math

4. Write a subtraction story about cheetahs.

   _____

   _____

Use with Lesson 6-11.

Name _____

Flat Surfaces, Vertices, and Edges

P 7-1

Write how many flat surfaces, vertices, and edges.
Then circle the objects that have the same shape.

1. A cube has __6__ flat surfaces, __8__ vertices, and __12__ edges.

2. A cylinder has ____ flat surfaces, ____ vertices, and ____ edges.

  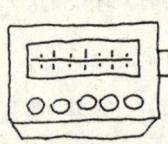 

3. A rectangular prism has ____ flat surfaces, ____ vertices, and ____ edges.

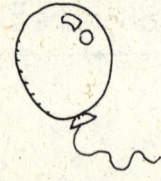   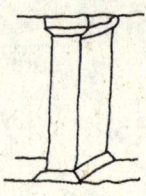

Problem Solving *Visual Thinking*

Circle the answer.

4. Which shapes could roll if you turned them on their side?

  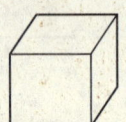 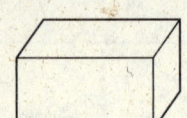

Use with Lesson 7-1.

Name _____

Relating Plane Shapes to Solid Figures   P 7-2

Circle the solid figure or figures you can trace to make the plane shape.

1.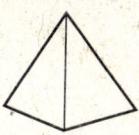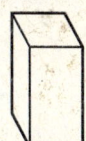
square

2.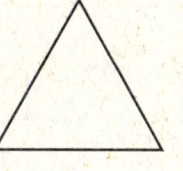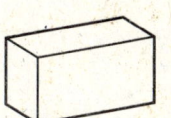
triangle

3.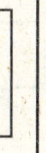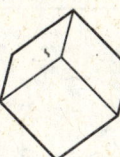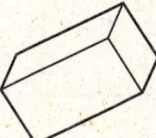
rectangle

4.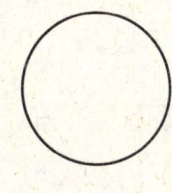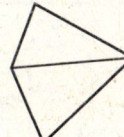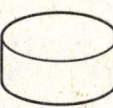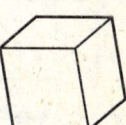
circle

Problem Solving *Algebra*

5. Count the number of vertices. Write a number sentence.

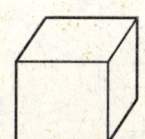 +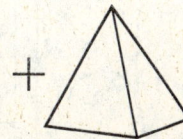

____ + ____ = ____

Use with Lesson 7-2.

Name _____

PROBLEM-SOLVING SKILL P 7-3

Use Data from a Picture

Circle the solid figure that the net will make if you fold it and tape it together.

1.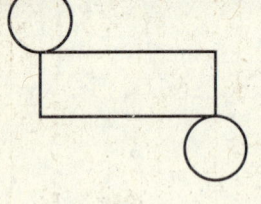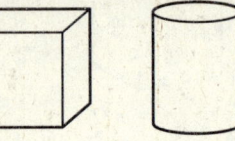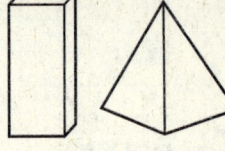

2.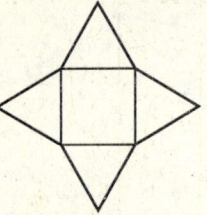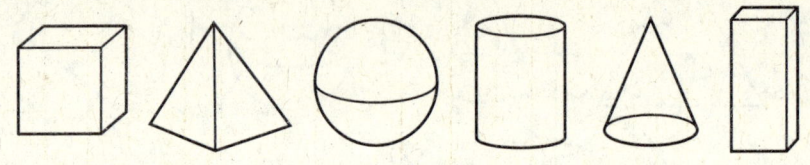

3.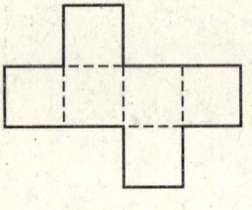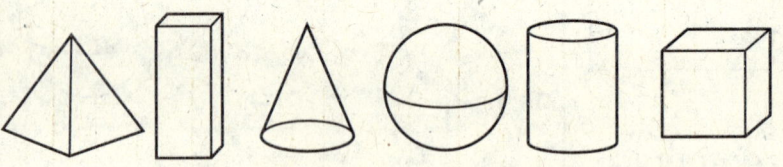

4.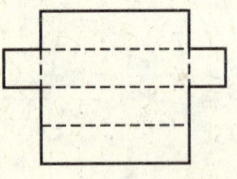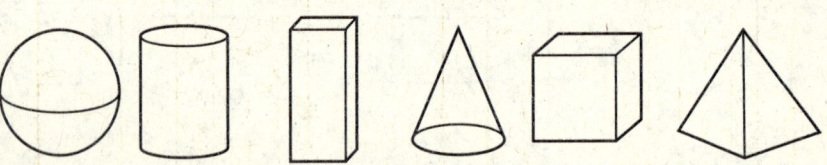

5.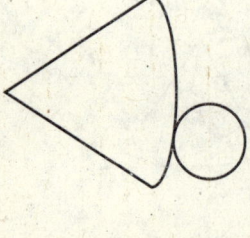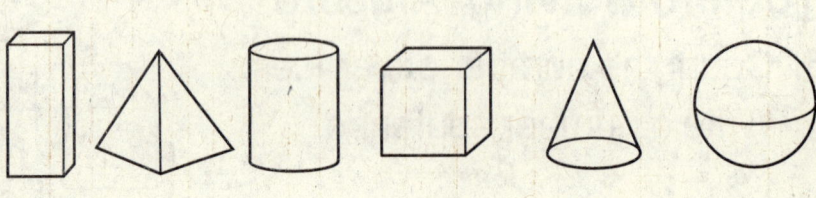

Name _____

Making New Shapes

P 7-4

Use pattern blocks to make the shape.
Trace and color to show one way to make it.
Write the number of sides and the number of angles.

1.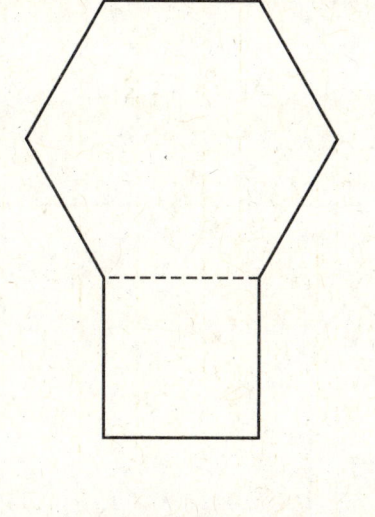

_____ sides _____ angles

2.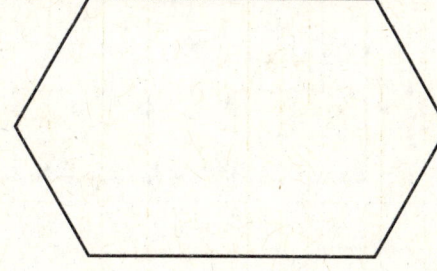

_____ sides _____ angles

Problem Solving *Visual Thinking*

3. Make these triangles with the number of pattern blocks shown.

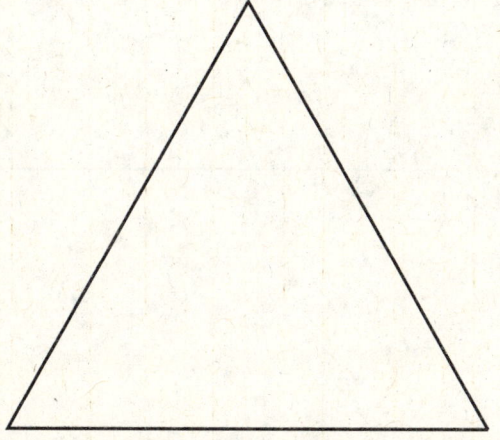

5 blocks

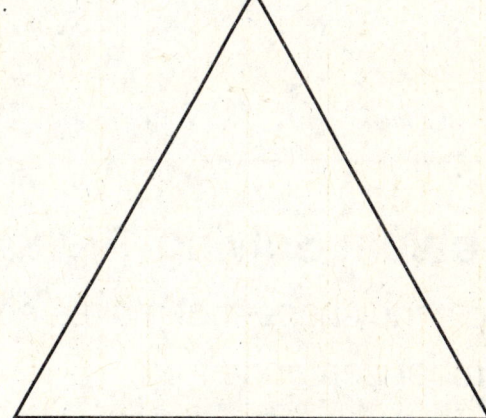

7 blocks

Use with Lesson 7-4. **81**

Name _____

P 7-5

Congruence

Draw a shape that is congruent.

1.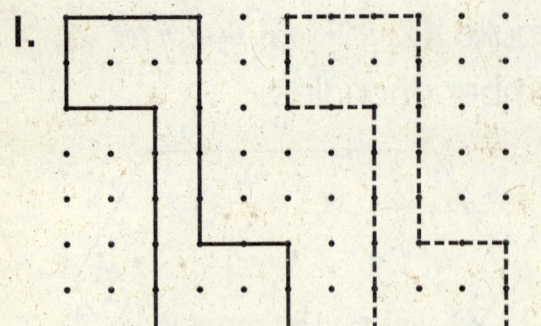

2.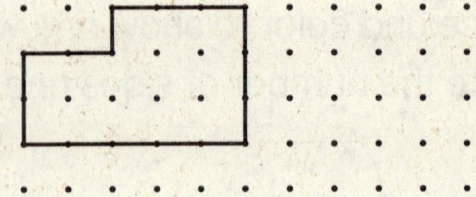

3.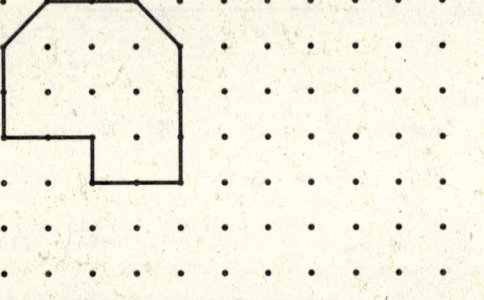

4.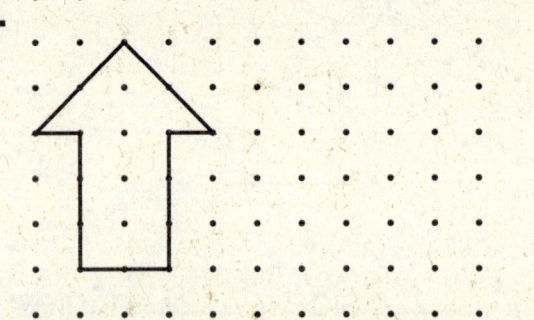

Draw shapes that are congruent.

5.

6.

Problem Solving *Algebra*

Draw the shape that makes each number sentence true.

☐ = 7   ◯ = 8   △ = 9

7. 8 + ___ = 17

8. 6 + ___ = 13

82 Use with Lesson 7-5.

Name _____

Slides, Flips, and Turns

P 7-6

Is it a slide, a flip, or a turn?
Circle the answer.

1.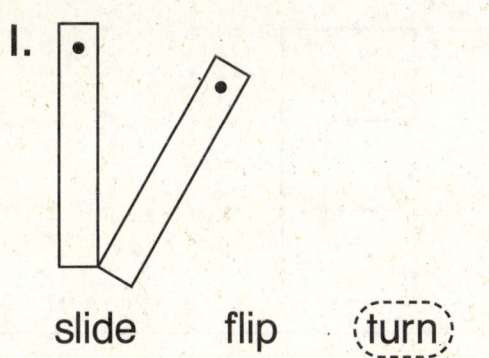

   slide   flip   (turn)

2.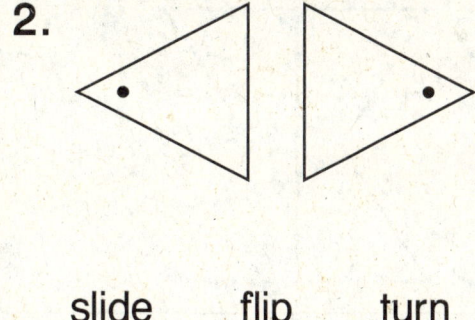

   slide   flip   turn

3.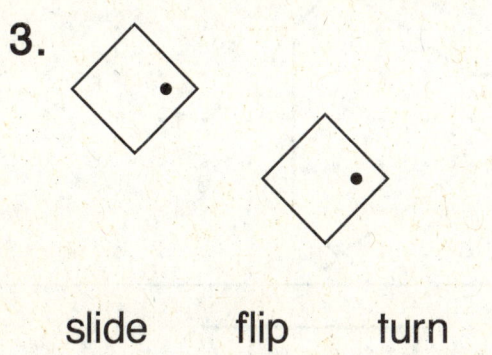

   slide   flip   turn

4.

   slide   flip   turn

5.

   slide   flip   turn

6.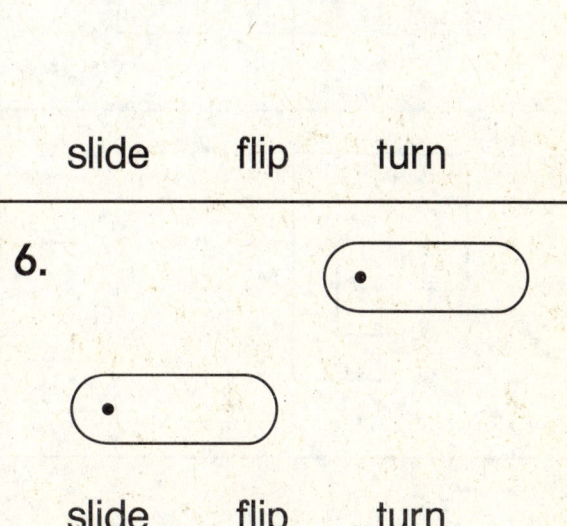

   slide   flip   turn

Problem Solving Visual Thinking

7. Look at the pattern.
   Draw the shape in its next position.
   Then circle the answer.

   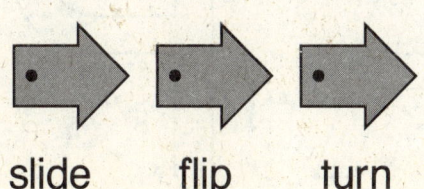

   slide   flip   turn

Use with Lesson 7-6.

Symmetry

Draw the matching part to make the shape symmetrical.

1.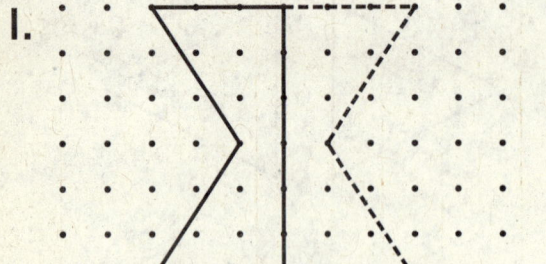
2.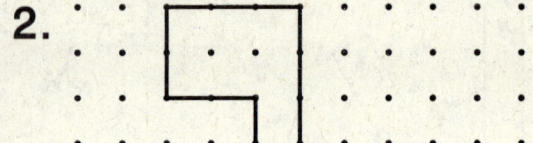
3.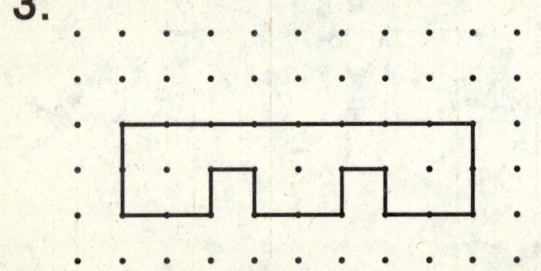
4.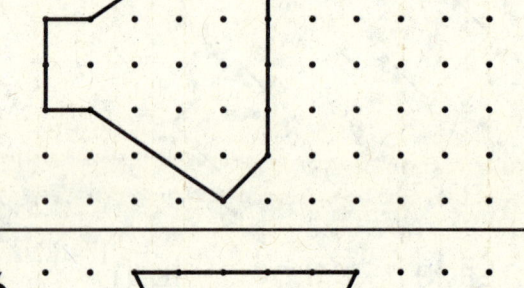
5.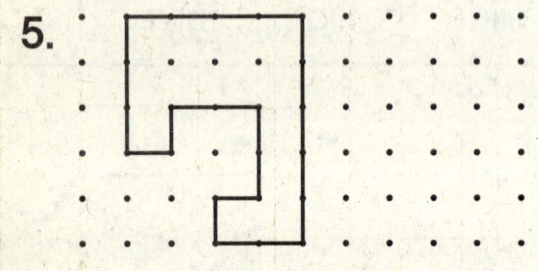
6.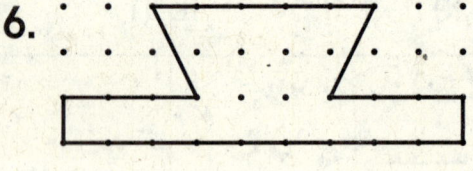

Problem Solving *Reasoning*

7. Draw as many lines of symmetry as you can. Circle any letter that does not have symmetry.

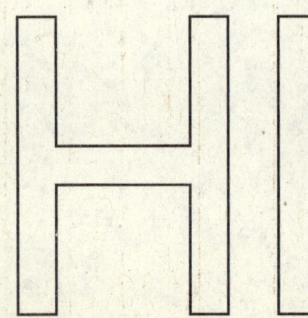 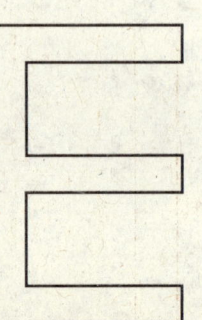  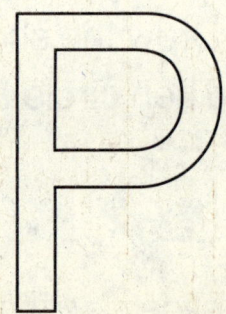

Name _____

PROBLEM-SOLVING STRATEGY P 7-8

Use Logical Reasoning

Cross out the shapes that do not fit the clues.
Circle the shape that answers the question.

1. Who am I?
   I have 4 angles.
   I have only 1 line
   of symmetry.

   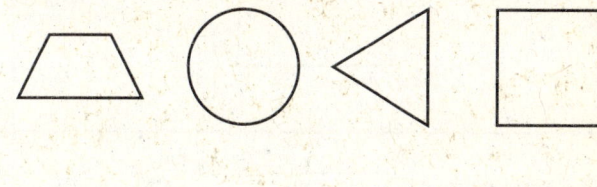

2. Who am I?
   I have 2 lines
   of symmetry.
   I have 4 angles.

   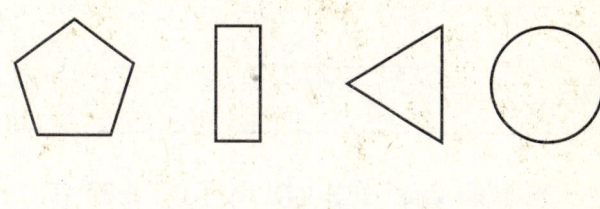

3. Who am I?
   I have more than 3 angles.
   I have 6 lines
   of symmetry.

   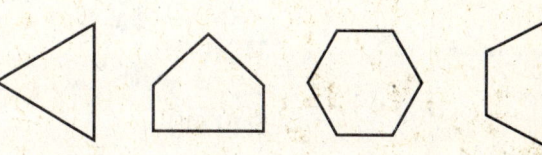

Problem Solving *Writing in Math*

4. Write a riddle about one of
   these solid shapes.
   Have a friend solve your riddle.

   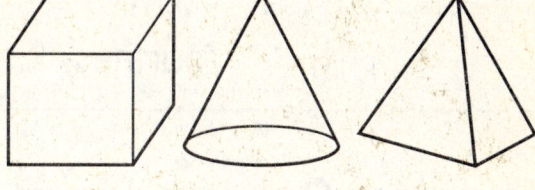

   _____
   _____
   _____
   _____

Use with Lesson 7-8. **85**

Name _____

Equal Parts

P 7-9

Draw a line or lines to show equal parts.

1. fourths
2. halves

3. thirds
4. fourths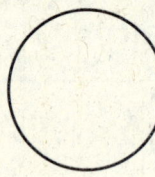

Does the picture show halves, thirds, or fourths?
Circle your answer.

5. 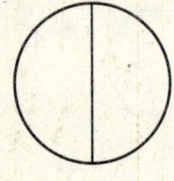   halves
   thirds
   fourths

6. 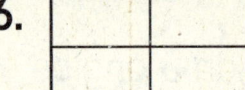   halves
   thirds
   fourths

7.    halves
   thirds
   fourths

8. 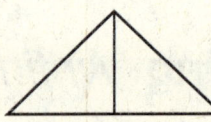   halves
   thirds
   fourths

Problem Solving *Visual Thinking*

9. Draw one more line to show fourths.

      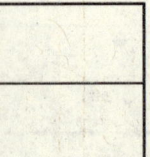

Name _____

Estimating Fractions

P 7-12

How much is left? Circle the best estimate.

1.    about $\frac{1}{2}$
   about $\frac{2}{3}$
   about $\frac{3}{4}$

2.    about $\frac{1}{5}$
   about $\frac{1}{2}$
   about $\frac{2}{4}$

3.    about $\frac{1}{4}$
   about $\frac{2}{5}$
   about $\frac{1}{2}$

4.    about $\frac{1}{2}$
   about $\frac{5}{8}$
   about $\frac{3}{4}$

Problem Solving Number Sense

Color the fraction that was eaten blue.
Color the fraction that is left red.

5. Beth and Tim eat $\frac{2}{3}$ of a pizza pie.

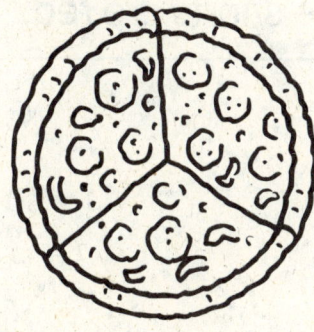

6. Maya, Kahli, and Rob eat $\frac{3}{5}$ of a loaf of bread.

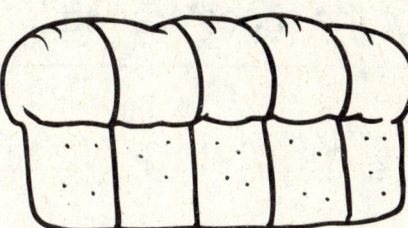

Use with Lesson 7-12.

Name _____

Fractions of a Set

P 7-13

Write the fraction of the group that is shaded.

1. 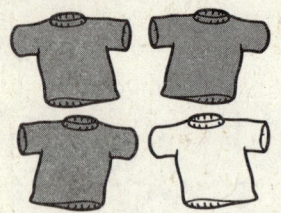 $\frac{3}{4}$

2.    ___

3.    ___

4.    ___

Color to show the fraction.

5.

$\frac{6}{8}$ of the socks are red.

6.

$\frac{7}{10}$ of the mittens are red.

7.

$\frac{1}{2}$ of the shoes are red.

8.

$\frac{3}{6}$ of the shorts are red.

Problem Solving *Number Sense*

Solve.

9. Sue has 9 baseball cards.

   She gives 4 cards to her brother.

   How many cards does Sue have left? _____

   What fraction of the cards does Sue have? _____

Name _____

PROBLEM-SOLVING APPLICATIONS P 7-14

Under the Sea

1. Here is a type of shell that is found in deep water. This shell can get up to 3 inches long. What shape do you think of when you look at this shell? I think of a

   _____

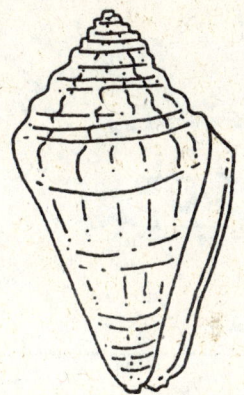

2. This shell is called a bi-valve. It means that there are two half-shells. How many lines of symmetry can you draw on the shells? Draw them.

   _____ line of symmetry

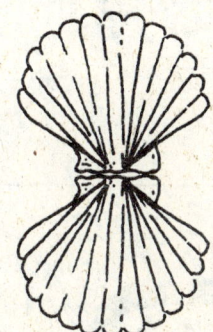

Writing in Math

3. Draw a picture of a shell that you have found or would like to find. Then write a sentence that describes its shape.

   _____

   _____

   _____

Telling Time to Five Minutes

P 8-1

Draw the clock hands for each time.

1.

2.

3.

4.

5.

6.

Problem Solving *Reasoning*

7. The time is 5:15. Is the hour hand closer to the 5 or the 6? Why?

_____

_____

Name _____

Telling Time After the Hour

P 8-2

Write the time or draw the minute hand to show the time. Circle another way to say the time.

1.     (20 minutes after 8)
   8 fifteen

2.     quarter past 1
   30 minutes after 1

3.     half past 11
   40 minutes after 11

4.     5 o'clock
   5 minutes after 5

Problem Solving *Reasoning*

5. Carly takes music lessons at 2:30. She arrives at quarter past 2. Is she early or late for her lesson? How do you know?

_____

_____

_____

Name _____

Telling Time Before the Hour

P 8-3

Write the time or draw the minute hand to show the time. Write the time before the hour.

1.   quarter to __8__

2.   25 minutes before ____

3.   10 minutes before ____

4.   5 minutes before ____

Problem Solving *Writing in Math*

5. Write two ways to say the time shown.

_____

_____

Name _____

Estimating Time

P 8-4

Match each activity to the amount of time it would take.

1. Coloring a picture

about 8 minutes

about 8 days

about 8 hours

2. Watering a garden

about 10 minutes

about 10 days

about 10 hours

3. Playing a ball game

about 2 minutes

about 2 days

about 2 hours

4. Making a sandwich

about 5 minutes

about 5 days

about 5 hours

5. Going camping

about 4 minutes

about 4 days

about 4 hours

6. Visiting a friend

about 3 minutes

about 3 days

about 3 hours

Problem Solving Number Sense

7. You and a friend play "Pass the Potato." How many times do you think you can pass the potato in one minute? Circle the better answer.

3 times   30 times

Name _____

Elapsed Time

P 8-5

Draw the clock hands and write the end time for each. Use a clock if you need to.

1. Cook dinner.   Starts   Lasts   Ends

 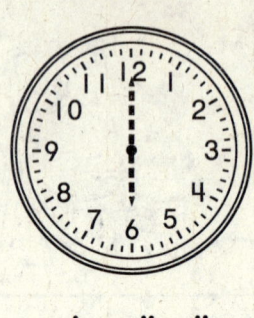

1 hour

5:00   6:00

2. Make your bed.

15 minutes

8:00   _____

Problem Solving *Number Sense*

3. Ricky leaves his house at 4:30.
   He rides his bike to the store for 15 minutes.

   What time does he get to the store? _____

Name _____

A.M. and P.M.

P 8-6

Draw lines to match the events to the times.

1.   2:00 A.M.   6:00 A.M.   4:00 P.M.

2.   8:00 P.M.   6:00 P.M.   11:00 A.M.

3.   3:00 P.M.   5:00 P.M.   8:00 A.M.

Problem Solving *Number Sense*

4. Sam helps his dad rake the yard at 11 A.M. He finishes at 1 P.M. How long did Sam rake the yard?

_____

5. Millie starts to read a book at 7:00 P.M. She reads for one hour and 30 minutes. What time did she finish reading?

_____

Use with Lesson 8-6.

Name _____

Using a Calendar

P 8-7

[Calendar for the year with all 12 months displayed]

Use the calendar to answer the questions.

1. What month comes just before April? _____

2. How many months have 31 days? _____

3. What month is the ninth month of the year? _____

4. What day of the week is December 3rd on this calendar? _____

5. What date follows June 30? _____

Problem Solving *Reasoning*

Use the calendar to solve.

6. Sara's birthday is in a month that has 5 Thursdays. Her birthday is on a Thursday, and is the 23rd of the month. What month is her birthday? _____

Name _____

Equivalent Times

P 8-8

Afternoon Schedule	
12:15–12:45	Music
12:45–1:45	Science
1:45–2:00	Recess
2:00–2:15	Story Time
2:15–2:45	Social Studies
2:45–3:00	Clean Up

Use the schedule to answer the questions.

1. Which two activities are one half hour long?

   _____

2. How many hours long is Science? _____

3. Name other activities that are as long as Recess.

   _____

4. How long are Story Time and Social Studies together?

   _____

Problem Solving *Visual Thinking*

5. Look at each clock. What activity takes place between these times?

   _____

Use with Lesson 8-8.   99

Name _____

PROBLEM-SOLVING STRATEGY   P 8-9

Make a Table

The second grade class drew pictures of their favorite pets. Complete the table. Use tally marks.

Favorite Pets	
Rabbit	
Dog	
Hamster	
Cat	
Bird	

1. How many children drew dogs as their favorite pet? _____ children

2. Do more children like hamsters or birds? _____
   How many more? _____ children

3. What pet is the favorite of most children? _____

4. Which pet did 1 child name as the favorite? _____

5. How many children are in this class? _____ children

6. What if some children drew these pictures as their favorite pets? Draw the tally marks there would be for turtles. _____

Name _____

Recording Data from a Survey

P 8-10

Use the survey to answer the questions.

Favorite Foods	
Food	Number of Children
Spaghetti	|||| |||| ||||
Hot dogs	|||| |||| |||| ||||
Cereal	|||| ||||	

1. How many children chose hot dogs? _____ children

2. Which food is the favorite of

   the greatest number of children? _____

3. How many more children chose

   spaghetti than cereal? _____ children

4. Which food did the least number

   of children choose? _____

Problem Solving Number Sense

Solve.

5. If 7 more children choose spaghetti,

   what will the new total be for spaghetti? _____ children

Use with Lesson 8-10. **101**

Name _____

Using a Venn Diagram

P 8-11

Ask 8 children the question below. Record the data using their names.

Do you like cats or dogs or both?

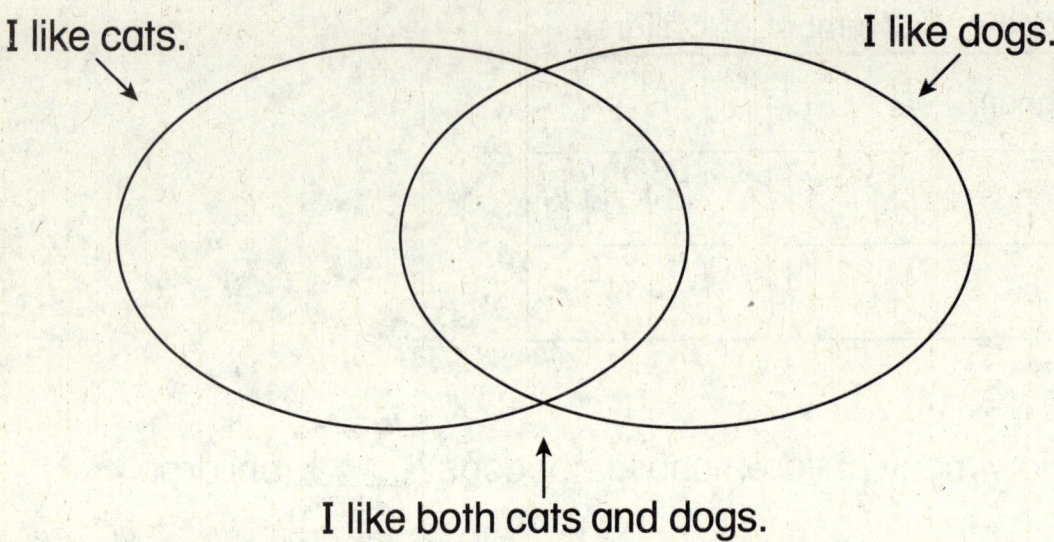

Use the diagram to answer the questions.

1. How many children like cats? _____ children

2. How many children like cats but not dogs? _____ children

3. How many children like dogs? _____ children

4. How many children like dogs but not cats? _____ children

Problem Solving *Writing in Math*

5. How can you use the diagram to tell how many children like both cats and dogs?

_____

_____

Name _____

Pictographs

P 8-12

Use the graphs to answer the questions.

Favorite TV Show

Animal Stories	🖥️🖥️🖥️🖥️ 🖥️🖥️🖥️
Sports	🖥️🖥️🖥️
Cartoons	🖥️🖥️🖥️🖥️ 🖥️🖥️🖥️🖥️ 🖥️🖥️🖥️

Each 🖥️ = 1 child

1. Which show is favored by most children?

   _____

2. How many children like Animal Stories best? ____

3. Which show is the favorite of 3 children? _____

Favorite Colors

	😊	
😊	😊	
😊	😊	
😊	😊	😊
😊	😊	😊
Red	Blue	Green

Each 😊 = 2 children

4. Which color is favored by most children?

   _____

5. How many children like red best?

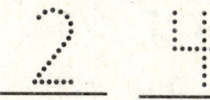

Problem Solving Number Sense

6. If 4 more children choose green, write a number sentence that tells how many children like green now. Solve.

_____

Use with Lesson 8-12. 103

Name _____

Bar Graphs

P 8-13

1. Take a survey. Ask classmates what they like to do inside. Make tally marks to keep track of what each classmate says.

Play games	
Play with toys	

2. Make a bar graph. Color one box for each time an activity was chosen.

Favorite Inside Activities

Activity										
Play games										
Play with toys										

Number of Children

Use the graph to answer each question.

3. Which activity is favored by the most children? _____

4. Which activity is favored by the least children? _____

Problem Solving *Writing in Math*

5. Explain how you read the information in the bar graph.

_____

_____

_____

Use with Lesson 8-13.

Name _____

Line Plots

P 8-14

Use the line plot to answer the questions.

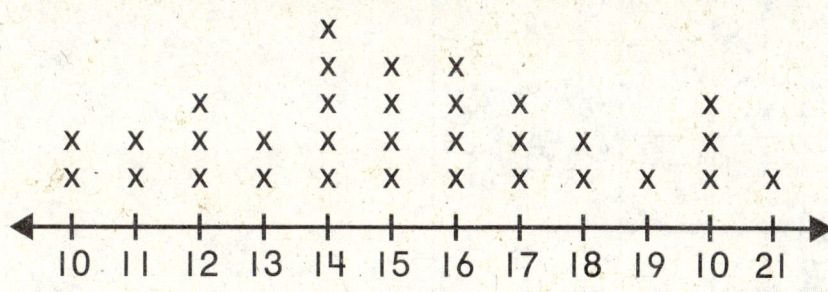

Number of Letters in Our Names

Number of Letters

1. How many children have 15 letters in their name?

   _____ children

2. What is the greatest number of letters in a child's name?

   _____ letters

3. How many children have 17 or more letters in their name?

   _____ children

4. How many children have 15 or fewer letters in their name?

   _____ children

Problem Solving *Reasonableness*

Circle the answer that is more reasonable.

5. Susan's last name has fewer letters than her first name. How many letters are in her name in all?

   5   9

6. Marshall has more letters in his last name than his first name. How many letters are in his name in all?

   8   20

Coordinate Graphs

Find the Wild Animals

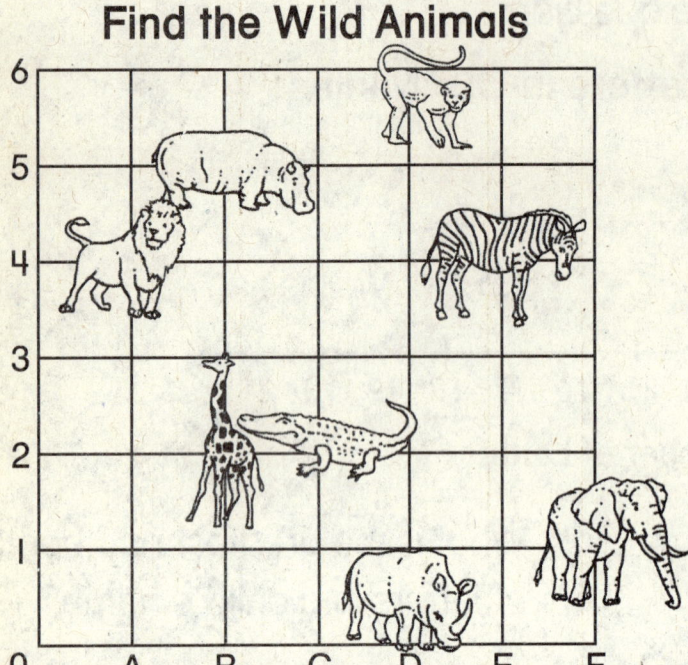

Write the ordered pair where each animal is located.

1.    (B, 5)

2.    _____

3.    _____

4.    _____

Problem Solving *Writing in Math*

5. Tell how you would find the ordered pair that tells the location of the lion.

_____

_____

_____

Name _____

PROBLEM-SOLVING SKILL P 8-16

Use Data from a Graph

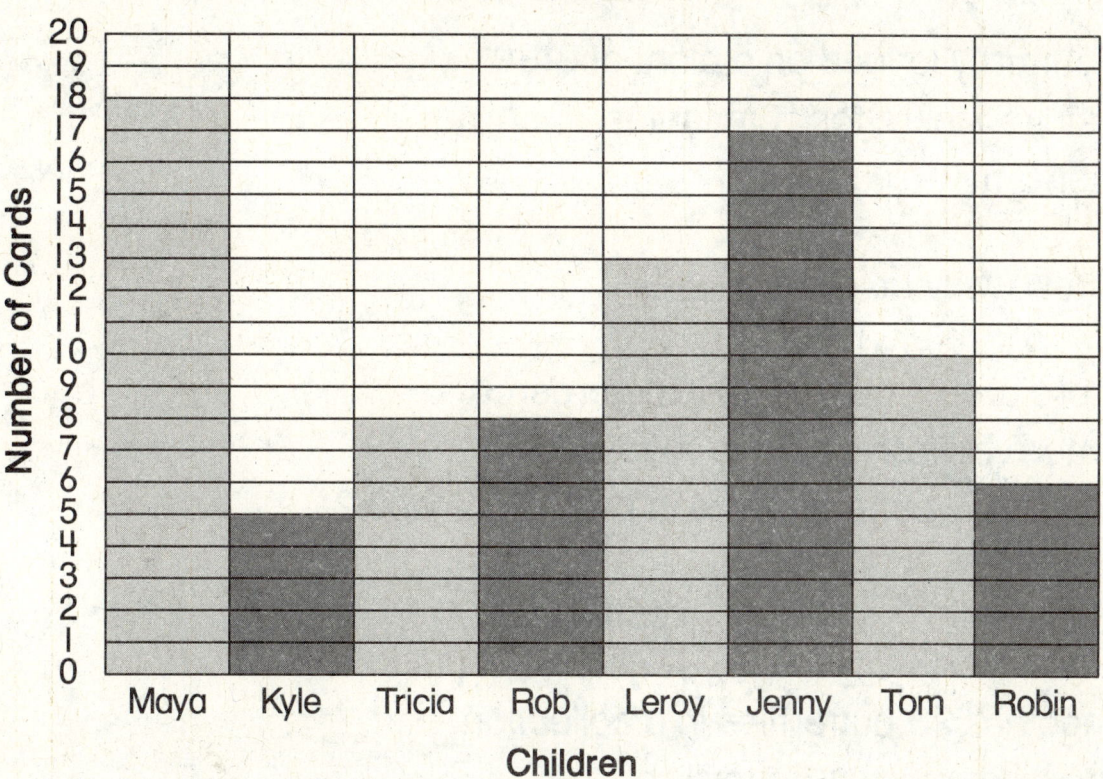

Use the graph to answer the questions.

1. Who has the most cards? _____

2. Who has the fewest? _____

3. Which two children have 8 cards? _____

4. Who has 13 cards? _____

Problem Solving *Reasonableness*

Circle the answer that makes sense.

5. Becky has more cards than Kyle and Leroy have altogether. How many cards could Becky have?

    15   7   25

Use with Lesson 8-16.

Name _____

PROBLEM-SOLVING APPLICATIONS　　　　　　　　　　P 8-17

Fly, Butterfly, Fly!

Solve.

1. A butterfly landed on a plant at 3:00.
   It stayed there for 10 minutes.
   Then it flew away.

   It flew away at ____ : ____ .

2. There are 17 butterflies in a garden.
   8 more butterflies come to join them.
   How many butterflies are in the garden now?

   ____ + ____ = ____ butterflies

3. Linda has 23 butterflies in a collection.
   She gives away 6 butterflies.
   How many butterflies are in her collection now?

   ____ ◯ ____ = ____ butterflies

Writing in Math

Write a story about a butterfly.

_____

_____

_____

_____

Use with Lesson 8-17.

Name _____

Understanding Length and Height

P 9-1

Measure each classroom object using cubes or paper clips. Circle the word or words that make sense.

1. 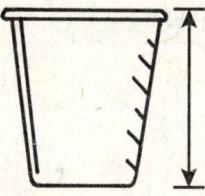 about _____ cubes / paper clips tall

2. 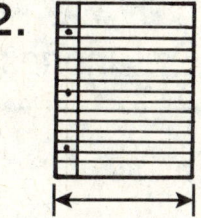 about _____ cubes / paper clips long

3.  about _____ cubes / paper clips long

4. 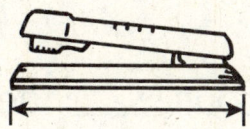 about _____ cubes / paper clips long

Problem Solving *Visual Thinking*

Circle the eraser that is the tallest.

5.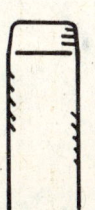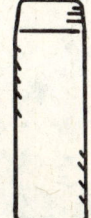

6.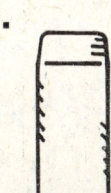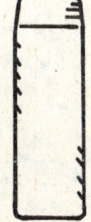

Name _____

Inches and Feet

P 9-2

Estimate the length or height of each object.
Then use a ruler to measure.

	Estimate.	Measure.
1. length of a desk	about _____ inches	about _____ inches
2. length of a crayon	about _____ inches	about _____ inches
3. height of a child	about _____ feet	about _____ feet

Problem Solving *Reasonableness*

Circle the better estimate for the length
or height of the object.

4.  The height of a thermos is

about 10 inches.

about 10 feet.

Name _____

Inches, Feet, and Yards

P 9-3

Estimate the width, height, or length of each object.
Then use a ruler or a yardstick to measure.

	Estimate.	Measure.
1. length of a chalkboard	about _____ feet	about _____ feet
2. height of a door	about _____ yards	about _____ yards
3. width of a chair	about _____ inches	about _____ inches

Problem Solving *Reasonableness*

Circle inches, feet, or yards.

4.  The bicycle is about 3 _____ tall.
   inches
   feet

5. 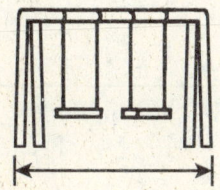 The swing set is about 3 _____ long.
   feet
   yards

Use with Lesson 9-3. **111**

Name _____

Centimeters and Meters

P 9-4

Estimate the length or height of each object.
Then use a ruler to measure.

	Estimate.	Measure.
1. length of a calendar	about ____ cm	about ____ cm
2. height of the wall	about ____ m	about ____ m
3. width of a pencil box	about ____ cm	about ____ cm

Problem Solving *Writing in Math*

4. Should Carla measure the length of the pool in centimeters or meters? Tell why you think so.

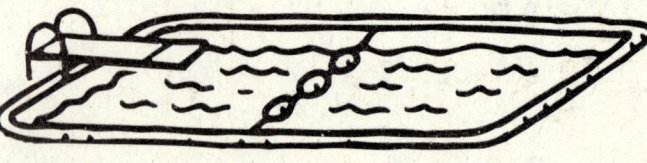

_____

_____

112 Use with Lesson 9-4.

Name _____

PROBLEM-SOLVING STRATEGY P 9-5

Act It Out

Find the perimeter and area of each shape.

1.

   perimeter: __8__ cm

   area: __4__ square units

2.

   perimeter: _____ cm

   area: _____ square units

3.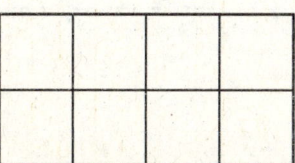

   perimeter: _____ cm

   area: _____ square units

4.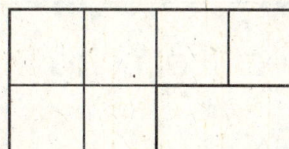

   perimeter: _____ cm

   area: _____ square units

Writing in Math

5. How can you find the number of square units inside of this parallelogram?

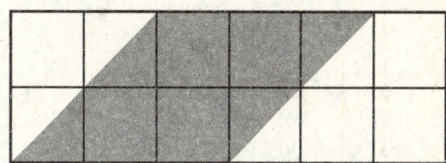

_____

_____

_____

Use with Lesson 9-5.

Name _____

Understanding Capacity

P 9-6

Circle the object that holds the most.

1.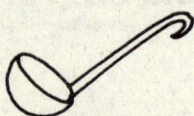

2.

3.

Circle the object that holds the least.

4.

5.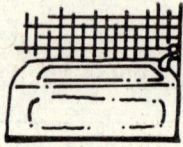

Problem Solving *Writing in Math*

6. Sally wants to water her garden. Circle the container she should use. Tell why.

Use with Lesson 9-6.

Name _____

Cups, Pints, and Quarts

P 9-7

Circle the containers that hold the same amount.

1.
2.
3.
4.

Problem Solving *Visual Thinking*

Use the pictures to answer the questions.

 =

Write **more than** or **less than**.

5. Does a gallon hold more or less than 2 quarts? _____
   How do you know?

   _____
   _____
   _____

6. Does a gallon hold more or less than 4 pints? _____
   How do you know?

   _____
   _____
   _____

Use with Lesson 9-7.

Name _____

P 9-8

Liters

About how many liters does the object hold?
Circle the better estimate.

1.

    about 30 liters

    (about 3 liters)

2.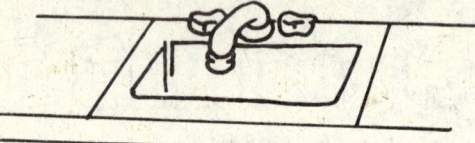

    about 10 liters

    about 2 liters

3.

    about 28 liters

    about 2 liters

4.

    about 9 liters

    about 90 liters

Problem Solving *Number Sense*

Solve.

5. How many 2 liter bottles of water can the cooler hold?

    12 liters   2 liters

    _____ bottles

Name _____

Understanding Volume

P 9-9

Circle the number of cubes in each box.

1. 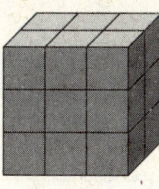   10 cubes   (18 cubes)

2. 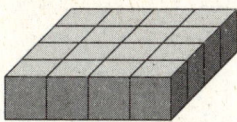   16 cubes   10 cubes

3. 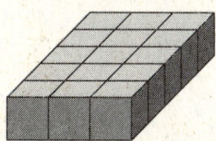   15 cubes   18 cubes

4. 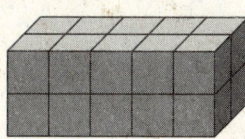   14 cubes   20 cubes

Problem Solving *Visual Thinking*

5. If 16 cubes fit into Jacinto's box, how many cubes do you think will fit into Elise's box?

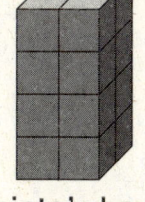 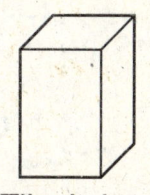

_____ cubes

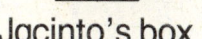

Jacinto's box   Elise's box

How do you know?

_____

_____

Use with Lesson 9-9. **117**

Name _____

Understanding Weight

P 9-10

Circle the object that weighs more.

1.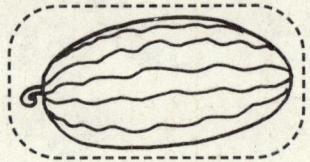

2.

3.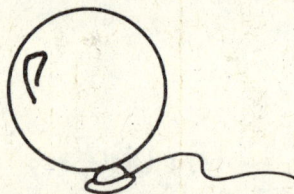

Circle the object that weighs less.

4.

5.

Problem Solving *Reasoning*

6. Name three objects that you think weigh more than an apple.

_____ _____ _____

118 Use with Lesson 9-10.

Pounds and Ounces

P 9-11

About how much does each object weigh?
Circle the better estimate.

1.
   (about 1 ounce)
   about 1 pound

2.
   about 2 ounces
   about 2 pounds

3.
   about 4 ounces
   about 4 pounds

4.
   about 12 ounces
   about 12 pounds

5.
   about 6 ounces
   about 6 pounds

6.
   about 10 ounces
   about 10 pounds

7.
   about 9 ounces
   about 9 pounds

8.
   about 5 ounces
   about 5 pounds

Problem Solving Algebra

Solve.

9. 1 pound is 16 ounces. How many ounces are in 2 pounds?

1 pound = 16 ounces
2 pounds = ? ounces

Name _____

Grams and Kilograms

P 9-12

About how much does each object measure?
Circle the better estimate.

1.
about 3 grams
(about 3 kilograms)

2.
about 60 grams
about 60 kilograms

3.
about 20 grams
about 20 kilograms

4.
about 400 grams
about 400 kilograms

5.
about 30 grams
about 30 kilograms

6.
about 8 grams
about 8 kilograms

Problem Solving Number Sense

Solve.

7. Circle the weight that will make both sides of the scale even.

1,000 g = 1 kg

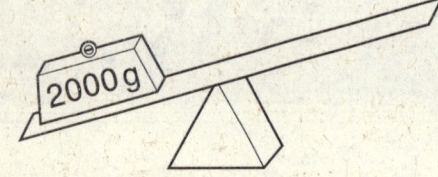

Use with Lesson 9-12.

Name _____

Temperature: Fahrenheit and Celsius   P 9-13

Color to show the temperature.
Circle **hot** or **cold** to tell about the temperature.

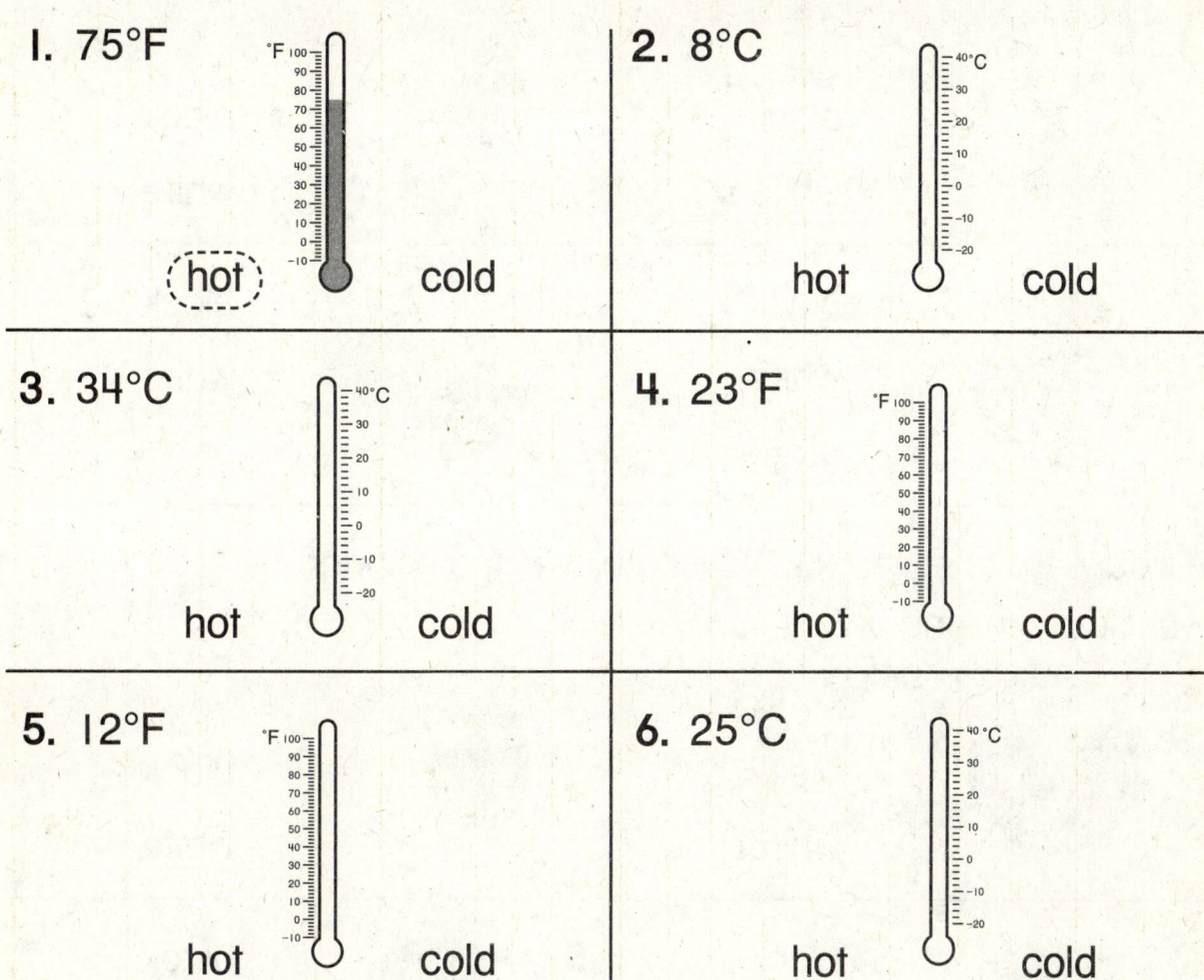

1. 75°F   (hot)   cold
2. 8°C   hot   cold
3. 34°C   hot   cold
4. 23°F   hot   cold
5. 12°F   hot   cold
6. 25°C   hot   cold

Problem Solving *Writing in Math*

7. Tell about the clothes you would wear if it were 35°F outside.

_____

_____

_____

Use with Lesson 9-13.

Name _____

Understanding Probability

P 9-14

If you were to spin once, which color is the spinner most likely to land on?

1.  black
   (white)

2.  black
   white

3. 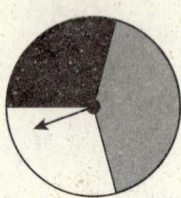 black
   white
   gray

4. 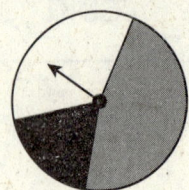 black
   white
   gray

If you were to spin once, which color is the spinner least likely to land on?

5. 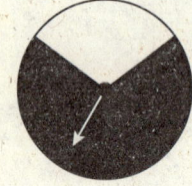 black
   white

6. 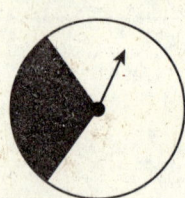 black
   white

7. 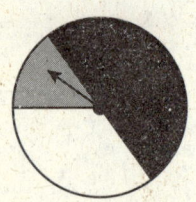 black
   white
   gray

8. 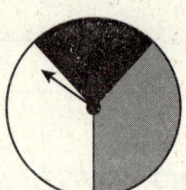 black
   white
   gray

Problem Solving *Reasoning*

Write more likely, less likely, or equally likely to answer the question.

9. Will the spinner land on black?

_____

Using Probability

P 9-15

Use the tally chart to help you answer the questions.
Circle the missing word to complete the sentence.

| Blue | |||| |||| | |
| Yellow | |||| |||| |||| |||| |

1. There are fewer _____ marbles in the jar.

   (blue)
   yellow

2. It is _____ that you will pick a red marble.

   certain
   impossible

3. It is _____ that you will pick a blue or yellow marble.

   probable
   certain

4. You can pick one marble. It is _____ that you will pick a yellow marble.

   probable
   impossible

Problem Solving *Reasoning*

5. There are red or yellow marbles in each jar.
   Color the marbles to match each description below each jar.

It is certain to pick a red marble.

It is impossible to pick a red marble.

Use with Lesson 9-15.

PROBLEM-SOLVING SKILL P 9-16
Multiple-Step Problems

Write a number sentence for each part of the problem.

1. Sam puts 8 cups of apple juice and 9 cups of grape juice in a party punch. How many cups are in the punch? _____ cups

   People at the party drink 11 cups of punch. How many cups of punch are left? _____ cups

2. A basket holds 21 pounds of tomatoes. Another basket holds 14 pounds of tomatoes. How many pounds of tomatoes are there altogether? _____ pounds

   Grandpa uses 16 pounds of tomatoes to make sauce. How many pounds of tomatoes are left? _____ pounds

Problem Solving *Mental Math*

Solve using mental math.

3. Beth has 20 red marbles and 15 blue marbles. Joyce has 40 yellow marbles. How many marbles do they have in all?

   _____ marbles

Name _____

PROBLEM-SOLVING APPLICATIONS P 9-17

How Do You Measure Up?

Is each object **heavier than, lighter than,** or **about** 1 pound?

Estimate. Then use a pound weight and a balance scale to check.

1.

   Estimate: _____ 1 pound

   Measure: _____ 1 pound

2.

   Estimate: _____ 1 pound

   Measure: _____ 1 pound

3. Some bananas weigh 3 pounds.
   A melon weighs 2 pounds.
   A bag of apples weighs 4 pounds.
   How much does the fruit weigh in all? _____ pounds

Writing in Math

4. Write a story about two pets you know.
   Then tell how much you think the animals weigh.

   _____

   _____

   _____

Building 1,000

Write how many. Use models if you need to.

1. 800 | 100 less is 700 | 100 more is 900
2. _____ | 100 less is _____ | 100 more is _____
3. _____ | 100 less is _____ | 100 more is _____
4. _____ | 100 less is _____ | 100 more is _____

Problem Solving *Algebra*

Write the number.

5. How many more hundreds do you need to make 500?

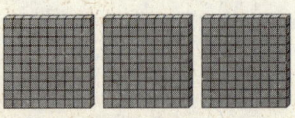

_____ + _____ = 500

Counting Hundreds, Tens, and Ones

P 10-2

Write the numbers.
Use models and Workmat 5 if you need to.

1.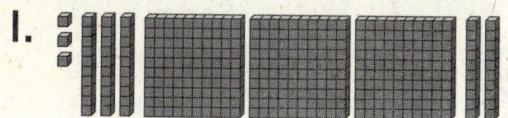

Hundreds	Tens	Ones
3	5	3	353

2.

Hundreds	Tens	Ones

3.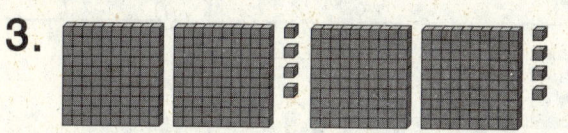

Hundreds	Tens	Ones

4.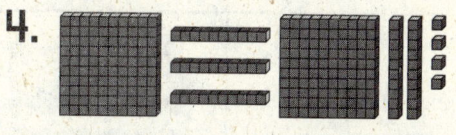

Hundreds	Tens	Ones

5.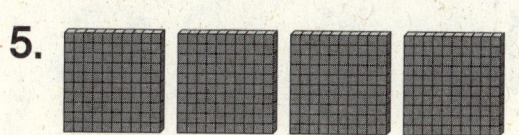

Hundreds	Tens	Ones

6.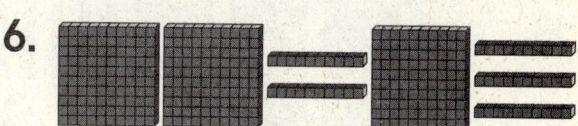

Hundreds	Tens	Ones

Problem Solving *Reasoning*

7. What is the greatest number you can make using these digits?

   5   7   2   _____

8. What is the smallest number you can make using these digits?

   3   1   8   _____

Use with Lesson 10-2.

Name _____

P 10-3

Writing Numbers to 1,000

Circle the models to match the expanded form.
Write the number in standard form.

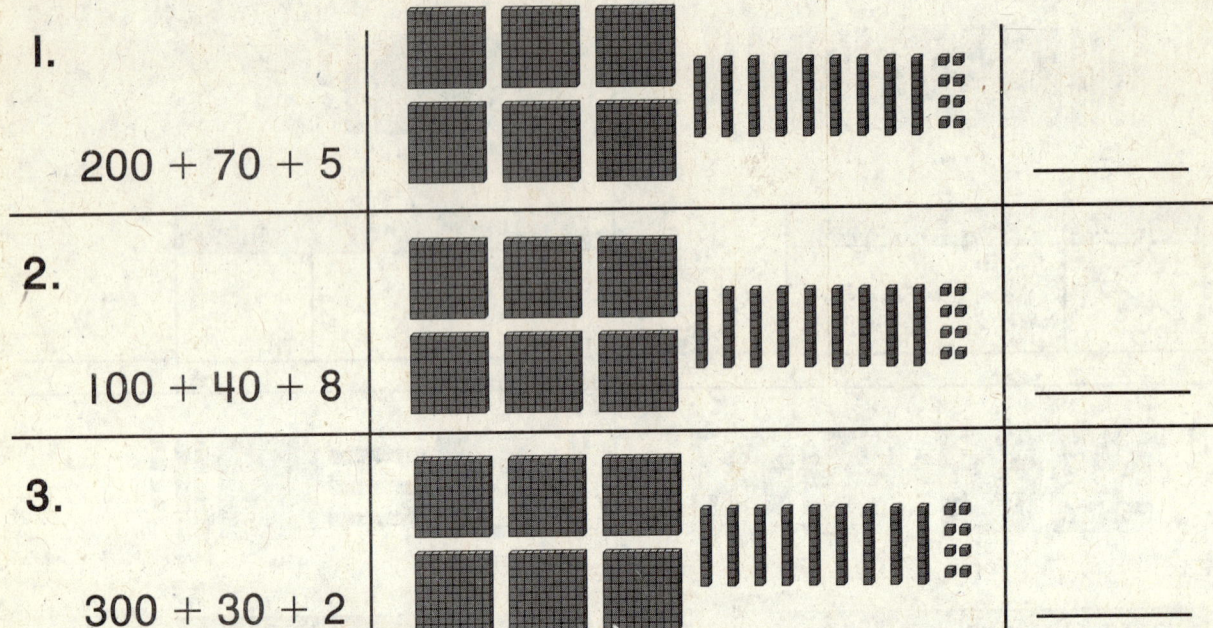

1. 200 + 70 + 5   _____

2. 100 + 40 + 8   _____

3. 300 + 30 + 2   _____

Circle the models to match the standard form.
Write the number in expanded form.

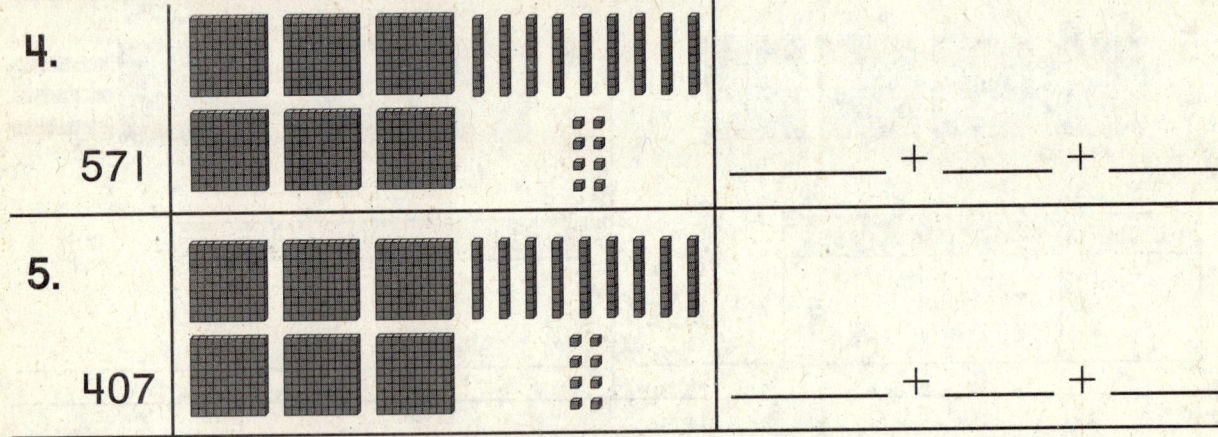

4. 571   ____ + ____ + ____

5. 407   ____ + ____ + ____

Problem Solving *Mental Math*

Write the total.

6. Crayons come in boxes of 10.
   How many boxes do you
   need for 100 crayons? _____ boxes

10 crayons = 1 box

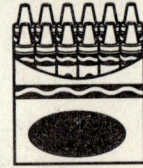

Name _____

Changing Numbers by Hundreds and Tens

P 10-4

Use models, drawings, or mental math to solve the problem.

1. 362 − 10 = _____

   362 − 100 = _____

2. 148 + 40 = _____

   148 + 400 = _____

3. 594 − 30 = _____

   594 − 300 = _____

4. 433 + 20 = _____

   433 + 200 = _____

Problem Solving Number Sense
Solve.

5. Mickey has 234 baseball cards. He gets 50 more cards. How many cards does he have now?

   _____ cards

6. Dixie has 426 baseball cards. She gives away 200 cards. How many cards does she have now?

   _____ cards

Name _____

Comparing Numbers

P 10-5

Compare. Write >, <, or =. Use models if you need to.

1. 157 ◯ 214   361 ◯ 378   419 ◯ 516

2. 600 ◯ 598   771 ◯ 771   645 ◯ 546

3. 197 ◯ 217   505 ◯ 550   987 ◯ 978

4. 384 ◯ 478   727 ◯ 582   408 ◯ 804

Problem Solving *Visual Thinking*

5. Draw lines to match the clues with the correct model.

My number is less than 5 hundreds. The ones digit is less than 7.

My number is greater than 3 hundreds. The tens digit is greater than 5.

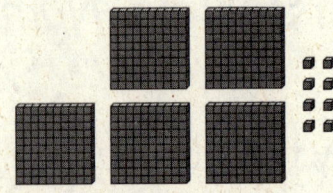

My number has more than 3 hundreds. There are 0 tens in the number.

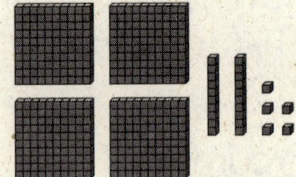

Name _____

Parts of 1,000

P 10-6

Count on to solve each problem.

1. Kayla has 850 points. How many more points does she need to get to 1,000?

    850 + __150__ = 1,000

    __150__ points

2. Abdul has 550 points. If he needs 1,000 points to win, how many more points does he need?

    550 + _____ = 1,000

    _____ points

3. Monty has 700 points. He needs 1,000 points to win. How many more points does he need?

    700 + _____ = 1,000

    _____ points

4. Suki has 350 points. How many more points does she need to get to 1,000?

    350 + _____ = 1,000

    _____ points

Problem Solving Number Sense

Find the missing number.

5. Misha has 250 points. Tasia has 300 points. They need 1,000 points to win. How many more points do they need?

    250 + 300 + __?__ = 1,000   _____ points

Use with Lesson 10-6.

Name _____

PROBLEM-SOLVING SKILL　　　　　　　　　　　　　　　P 10-7

Use Data from a Chart

Use data from the chart to answer the questions.

Number of People at the Games	
Basketball	465
Baseball	390
Soccer	288
Hockey	432

1. Did more people come to the baseball game or the hockey game? _____

2. Which game did 400 + 60 + 5 people come to watch? _____

3. 2 hundreds, 8 tens, and 8 ones tells how many people came to which game? _____

Problem Solving *Reasonableness*

Circle the number that makes the most sense.

4. About $\begin{array}{c}50\\500\end{array}$ people are watching basketball.

5. About $\begin{array}{c}300\\30\end{array}$ people are watching soccer.

Circle the words that make more sense.

6. The number of people at a basketball game is _____ the number of people at a hockey game.　　less than / greater than

Before, After, and Between

P 10-8

Write the number that comes after.

1. 235, _____   489, _____   600, _____

2. 319, _____   899, _____   534, _____

Write the number that comes before.

3. _____, 730   _____, 405   _____, 337

4. _____, 800   _____, 179   _____, 298

Write the number that comes between.

5. 375, _____, 377   819, _____, 821   197, _____, 199

6. 199, _____, 201   450, _____, 452   834, _____, 836

Write the number.

7. What is one before 278? _____

8. What is one after 743? _____

9. What number is between 681 and 683? _____

Problem Solving *Reasoning*

Circle the numbers.

10. Which two numbers come after 297?   213   307   299

11. Which two numbers come before 810?   775   801   811

12. Which two numbers come between 400 and 450?   425   465   419

Use with Lesson 10-8. **133**

Name _____

Ordering Numbers

P 10-9

Write the numbers in order from least to greatest.

1. 673, 628, 515, 437, 321

   <u>321</u>, <u>437</u>, <u>515</u>, <u>628</u>, <u>673</u>

2. 423, 409, 457, 524, 582

   _____, _____, _____, _____, _____

3. 507, 387, 652, 481, 658

   _____, _____, _____, _____, _____

4. 198, 277, 156, 287, 192

   _____, _____, _____, _____, _____

Write the numbers in order from greatest to least.

5. 731, 682, 432, 819, 688

   _____, _____, _____, _____, _____

6. 331, 287, 207, 432, 211

   _____, _____, _____, _____, _____

Problem Solving Writing in Math

Use the space on the right to solve the problems.

7. In the numbers 572 to 592, are there more even or odd numbers? How do you know?

_____

_____

Use with Lesson 10-9.

Name _____

PROBLEM-SOLVING STRATEGY P 10-10
Look for a Pattern

Write the missing numbers. Describe the pattern.

1. 185, 195, 205, 215, _____, _____, _____

_____

_____

Write the number that is 50 less.

2.   778   690   187   958

   _____   _____   _____   _____

   What pattern do you see? _____

Write the number that is 300 more.

3.   205   537   169   649

   _____   _____   _____   _____

   What pattern do you see? _____

Problem Solving *Reasoning*

Find the pattern. Circle the number that comes next.

4. 105, 125, 145, 165   166   185   175

5. 300, 325, 350, 375   500   476   400

6. 550, 600, 650, 700   725   750   800

Use with Lesson 10-10.

Name _____

PROBLEM-SOLVING APPLICATIONS P 10-11
Rescue Vehicles

1. A fire truck traveled 267 miles in one month to put out fires. Record the number of hundreds, tens, and ones in 267.

   _____ hundreds   _____ tens   _____ ones

2. A fire boat had 215 calls in one year.
   It had 198 calls the next year.
   Compare these two numbers. Write >, <, or =.

   215 ◯ 198

3. A fire truck responded to an alarm at quarter past 10. What is another way to write this time?

   _____ : _____

Writing in Math

4. Write a number story about an ambulance. Use four numbers between 200 and 300. At the end of your story, list the numbers in order from greatest to least.

   _____

   _____

   _____

   _____

136 Use with Lesson 10-11.

Using Mental Math

P 11-1

Add. Use mental math.

1. 306 + 213 = _____   515 + 262 = _____

2. 164 + 311 = _____   623 + 123 = _____

3. 412 + 250 = _____   322 + 146 = _____

4. _____ = 303 + 404   711 + 105 = _____

5. 271 + 320 = _____   _____ = 319 + 120

6. 409 + 230 = _____   725 + 114 = _____

Problem Solving *Algebra*

Write the missing number that makes the number sentence true.

7. 400 + 500 = 600 + _____	8. 200 + _____ = 700 + 200
9. 300 + 200 = 0 + _____	10. 500 + 400 = 900 + _____
11. 100 + 700 = 400 + _____	12. 600 + _____ = 800 + 100

Use with Lesson 11-1. **137**

Estimating Sums

P 11-2

Is the sum more or less than the number?
Estimate the sum. Then write **more than** or **less than**.

1. Is 283 + 250 more than or less than 500? _____ 500

2. Is 415 + 403 more than or less than 850? _____ 850

3. Is 367 + 298 more than or less than 650? _____ 650

4. Is 454 + 432 more than or less than 900? _____ 900

5. Is 277 + 519 more than or less than 750? _____ 750

Problem Solving *Number Sense*

Look at the cards. Choose a number that will make each sentence true.

6. 382 + _____ is about 600.

7. 378 + _____ is less than 600.

8. 211 + _____ is more than 600.

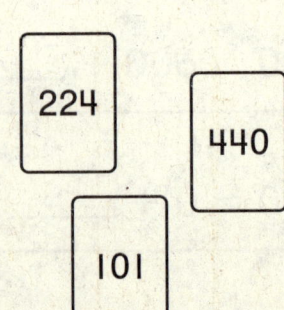

138 Use with Lesson 11-2.

Name _____

Adding with Models

P 11-3

Use models and Workmat 5. Show each number.
Add to find the sum.

1. 407 + 188 = _____

2. 182 + 253 = _____

3. 270 + 319 = _____

4. _____ = 558 + 127

5. 376 + 508 = _____

6. _____ = 194 + 233

Problem Solving *Estimation*

Circle the best estimate.

7.
Grade	Number of Children
1	235
2	189

About how many children are in both grades?

300   400   500

8.
Grade	Number of Children
3	429
4	311

About how many children are in both grades?

600   700   800

9. Each floor of the school holds 145 children. About how many children can the school hold if there are 2 floors?

150   250   300

Use with Lesson 11-3.   **139**

Name _____

Adding Three-Digit Numbers

P 11-4

Add. Use models and Workmat 5 if you need to.

1.

Hundreds	Tens	Ones
☐	☐	
6	3	4
+ 1	5	9

Hundreds	Tens	Ones
☐	☐	
1	2	9
+ 4	9	0

2. 457   219   405   286   124
   +138   +390   +263   +491   +209

Problem Solving *Number Sense*

3. For the problems, use each number for only one digit.

3   5   6   2   4   1

Make the greatest sum.   Make the least sum.

   2 7 2   2 7 2
 + ☐ ☐ ☐   + ☐ ☐ ☐
   ☐ ☐ ☐   ☐ ☐ ☐

Use with Lesson 11-4.

Name _____

Practice with Three-Digit Addition

P 11-5

Write the addition problem. Find the sum.

1. 291 + 105   315 + 482   158 + 771

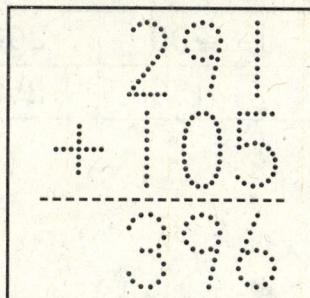  

2. 463 + 142   37 + 517   428 + 149

3. 219 + 168   537 + 92   502 + 238

Problem Solving Number Sense

Solve the number riddles.

4. When I am added to 210, the sum is 864.
   What number am I? _____

5. When I am added to 103, the sum is 333.
   What number am I? _____

Use with Lesson 11-5. 141

PROBLEM-SOLVING STRATEGY

Make a Graph

Use the chart to answer the questions.

Art Supplies			
	Crayons	Paints	Brushes
Art Room 1	350	200	300
Art Room 2	400	150	250

1. How many crayons are there in all?

   _____ crayons

2. How many paints are there in all? _____ paints

3. How many brushes are there in all? _____ brushes

4. Use your answers from Exercises 1–3 to complete the graph. Color to show how many of each of the art supplies there are in all.

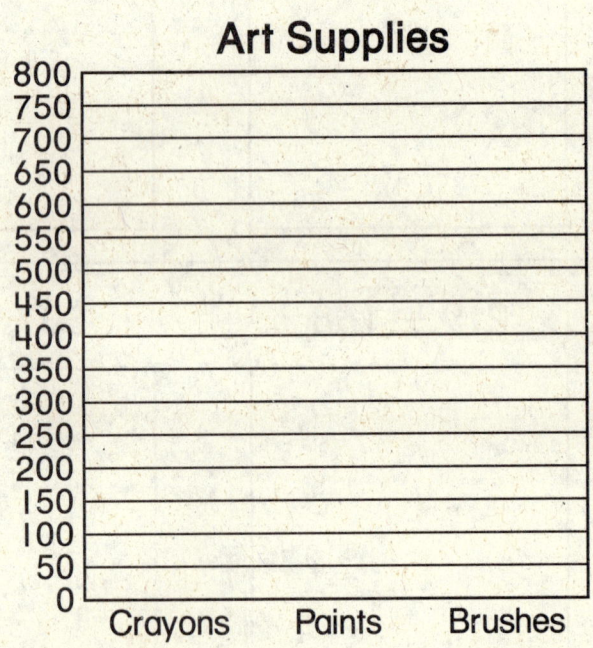

Problem Solving *Writing in Math*

5. How is a bar graph different from a chart?

   _____

   _____

Ways to Find Missing Parts

P 11-7

Count on or count back to find the missing part.

1. 360 + _____ = 600
2. 420 + _____ = 700
3. 180 + _____ = 700
4. 500 = 170 + _____
5. 270 + _____ = 900
6. 420 + _____ = 600
7. 700 = 390 + _____
8. 500 = _____ + 140

Problem Solving *Algebra*

Circle the weights you would need to balance each scale.

9.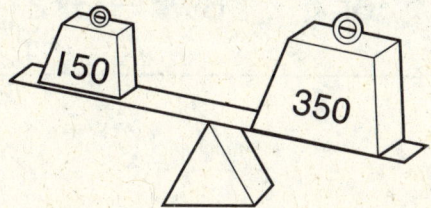

10.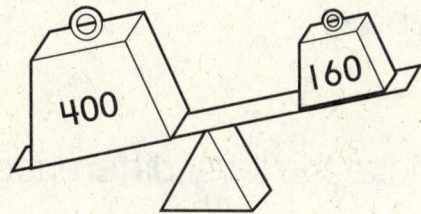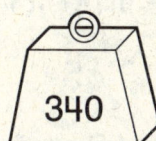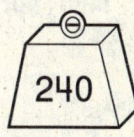

11.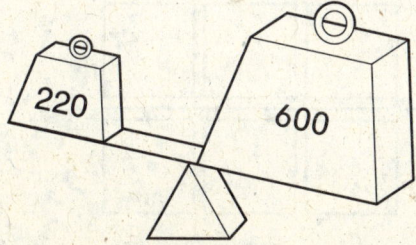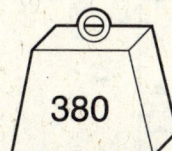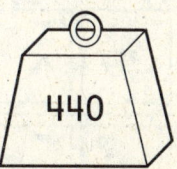

Estimating Differences

P 11-8

Circle the problem that matches the estimate.

1. about 400	718 − 487	or	921 − 513
2. about 200	933 − 567	or	478 − 301
3. about 100	684 − 572	or	376 − 123
4. about 500	834 − 311	or	769 − 487
5. about 300	659 − 147	or	801 − 490
6. about 600	714 − 588	or	899 − 312

Problem Solving *Number Sense*

For the problems, choose a set of 3 numbers.
Use each number one time. Subtract to solve.

2 5 7 1 4 6

7. Make the greatest difference.   8. Make the least difference.

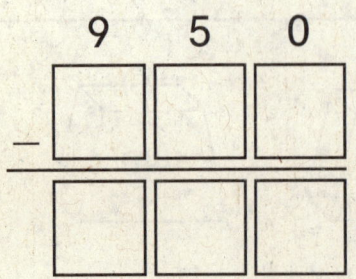
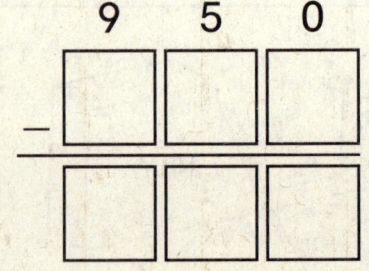

144 Use with Lesson 11-8.

Subtracting with Models

Subtract. Use models and Workmat 5.

1. 476 − 321 = _____
2. 659 − 372 = _____
3. 953 − 209 = _____
4. _____ = 561 − 442
5. 390 − 126 = _____
6. 732 − 121 = _____
7. _____ = 578 − 292
8. 818 − 409 = _____

Problem Solving *Reasoning*

9. Write the name of each child below the cards he or she collects.

Sports Card Collection

- Jake has about 300 more cards than Cindi.
- Melba has the most cards.
- William has about 100 less cards than Melba.

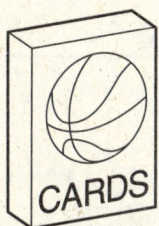   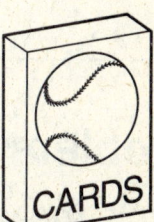

600 cards   200 cards   705 cards   510 cards

_____ _____ _____ _____

Name _____

Subtracting Three-Digit Numbers

P 11-10

Subtract. Use models and Workmat 5 if you need to.

1.

Hundreds	Tens	Ones
☐	☐	☐
7	8	4
− 2	5	1

Hundreds	Tens	Ones
☐	☐	☐
4	8	5
− 1	3	9

2.

Hundreds	Tens	Ones
☐	☐	☐
5	7	8
− 2	9	7

Hundreds	Tens	Ones
☐	☐	☐
6	2	4
− 3	3	2

3. 657   561   809   742   927
   −128   −390   −263   −450   −304

Problem Solving *Visual Thinking*

Circle the weight you need to remove to balance the scale.

4.

146 Use with Lesson 11-10.

Name _____

Practice with Three-Digit Subtraction   P 11-11

Write the subtraction problem. Find the difference.

1. 639 − 218   562 − 129   947 − 351

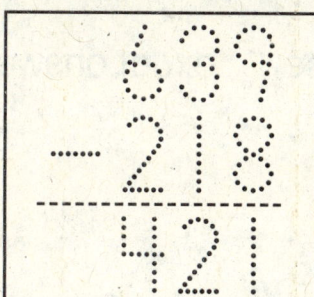  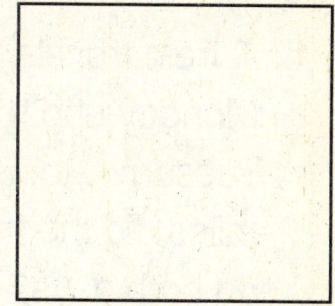

2. 817 − 253   707 − 95   478 − 321

3. 589 − 193   643 − 228   850 − 49

Problem Solving *Estimation*

Circle the best estimate.

4. 624 − 410 | 5. 934 − 411 | 6. 776 − 187
   100 200 300 | 500 600 700 | 400 500 600

Use with Lesson 11-11. **147**

Name _____

PROBLEM-SOLVING SKILL

P 11-12

Exact Answer or Estimate

Circle **estimate** or **exact answer**.
Answer the question.

1. A train travels 312 miles on Monday and 478 miles on Tuesday. About how many miles did the train travel on both days?

   estimate   exact answer

   _____

2. There are 517 children at the Elm Street school. 325 children take the bus to school. How many children do not take the bus to school?

   estimate   exact answer

   _____

3. Mrs. Cook reads a book with 572 pages. She has read about 300 pages. About how many pages does she have left to read?

   estimate   exact answer

   _____

Problem Solving *Writing in Math*

4. Write a math problem in which an exact answer is needed. _____

148   Use with Lesson 11-12.

Name _____

PROBLEM-SOLVING APPLICATIONS P 11-13

Amazing Animals

Solve.

1. A monkey sits on a tree that is 115 feet high. The monkey climbs 60 feet. Then it climbs another 50 feet. How high is the monkey now?

   _____ feet

2. One week, a group of chimpanzees ate 500 bananas. The next week, they ate 300 bananas. How many more bananas did the chimpanzees eat in the first week?

   _____ more bananas

3. A toucan sits on a branch that is 212 feet high. Another toucan sits on a branch that is 108 feet high. How much higher is the first toucan?

   _____ feet higher

Writing in Math

4. Write a subtraction story about your favorite rain forest animal. Use three-digit numbers in your story.

   _____

   _____

   _____

Use with Lesson 11-13.

Name _____

P 12-1

Skip Counting Equal Groups

Draw to show equal groups. Skip count to find how many there are in all. Use counters if you need to.

1. 2 groups, 5 in each group

 10 ____ in all

2. 5 groups, 3 in each group

____ in all

3. 4 groups, 2 in each group

____ in all

4. 3 groups, 2 in each group

____ in all

Problem Solving Writing in Math

Describe the skip counting pattern you use to find how many in all.

5.

_____

6.

_____

Use with Lesson 12-1.

Repeated Addition and Multiplication

P 12-2

Write an addition sentence and a multiplication sentence that tell how many there are in all.

1. (2 crayons) (2 crayons) (2 crayons)

   ___ + ___ + ___ = ___   ___ × ___ = ___

2. (2 pins) (2 pins) (2 pins) (2 pins)

   ___ + ___ + ___ + ___ = ___   ___ × ___ = ___

3. (3 paperclips) (3 paperclips) (3 paperclips) (3 paperclips)

   ___ + ___ + ___ + ___ = ___   ___ × ___ = ___

4. (6 circles) (6 circles) (6 circles)

   ___ + ___ + ___ = ___   ___ × ___ = ___

5. (6 erasers) (6 erasers)

   ___ + ___ = ___   ___ × ___ = ___

Problem Solving *Number Sense*

6. Find the sum. Write a multiplication sentence that shows the same amount.

   5 + 5 + 5 + 5 + 5 + 5 = ___   ___ × ___ = ___

Use with Lesson 12-2. **151**

Name _____

Building Arrays

P 12-3

Write a multiplication sentence to describe each array.

1.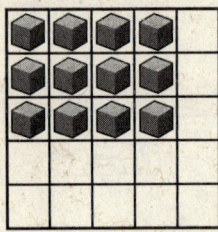

___ × ___ = ___
rows   in each   in all
       row

2.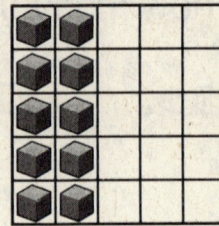

___ × ___ = ___

3.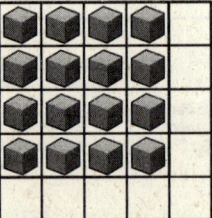

___ × ___ = ___

4.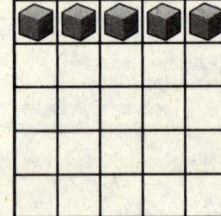

___ × ___ = ___

5.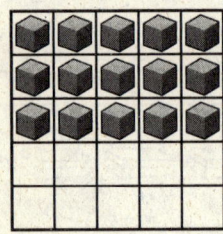

___ × ___ = ___

6.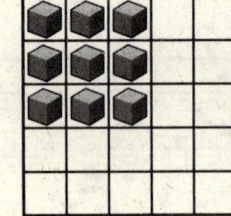

___ × ___ = ___

Problem Solving *Visual Thinking*

7. Write the multiplication sentence for the shaded squares.

   ___ × ___ = ___

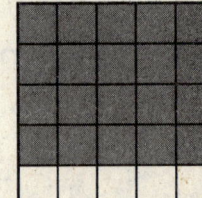

Use with Lesson 12-3.

Name _____

Multiplying in Any Order

P 12-4

Write the numbers. Multiply to find the product.

1. _____ rows 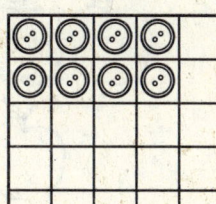   _____ rows

   _____ in each row   _____ in each row

   _____ × _____ = _____   _____ × _____ = _____

2. _____ rows 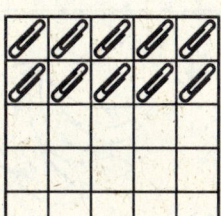   _____ rows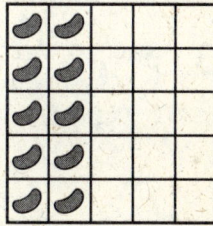

   _____ in each row   _____ in each row

   _____ × _____ = _____   _____ × _____ = _____

Problem Solving *Algebra*

Complete the number sentences.

3.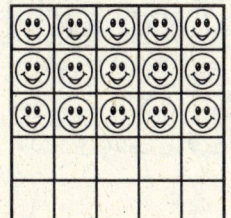

   3 × _____ = 15   5 × _____ = 25

Use with Lesson 12-4. **153**

Name _____

P 12-5

Vertical Form

Multiply across and down.

1.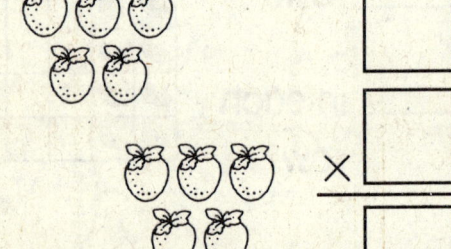

   ___4___ × ___3___ = ___12___

2.

   _____ × _____ = _____

3.

   _____ × _____ = _____

4.

   _____ × _____ = _____

Problem Solving Reasoning

5. Beth has 8 stickers.
   Write 2 multiplication sentences
   that tell different ways to group them.

   _____ × _____ = _____

   _____ × _____ = _____

154 Use with Lesson 12-5.

Name _____

PROBLEM-SOLVING STRATEGY　　　　　　　　　P 12-6
Draw a Picture

Draw a picture to solve each problem.
Then write a multiplication sentence.

1. Margot has 4 pencil holders.
   Each one holds 3 pencils.
   How many pencils does Margot have?

   _____ × _____ = _____ pencils

2. Ramona has 5 dolls.
   Each doll has 3 buttons.
   How many buttons are there in all?

   _____ × _____ = _____ buttons

3. Ben has 6 toy cars.
   Each car has 4 wheels.
   How many wheels are there in all?

   _____ × _____ = _____ wheels

Problem Solving *Estimation*

4. Jeb has 3 boxes with 7 crayons in each box.
   Does he have more or less than 18 crayons?
   Explain your answer.

   _____

   _____

Use with Lesson 12-6.　**155**

Making Equal Groups

P 12-7

How many coins will each child get?
Write the answer. Use coins if you need to.

1. 15 pennies, 5 children   Each child gets _____ pennies.

2. 20 nickels, 4 children   Each child gets _____ nickels.

3. 12 quarters, 3 children   Each child gets _____ quarters.

Complete the table.

	Number of coins	Number of children	How many coins does each child get?
4.	16	2	_____
5.	9	3	_____
6.	16	4	_____
7.	14	7	_____

Problem Solving *Number Sense*

8. You have 18 plums. Can you find 6 different ways to show equal groups?

_____ group of _____   _____ groups of _____

_____ groups of _____   _____ groups of _____

_____ groups of _____   _____ groups of _____

Use with Lesson 12-7.

Name _____

Writing Division Sentences

P 12-8

Draw to show equal groups. Write the division sentence.

1. 9 markers divided among 3 boxes.

   ___ ÷ ___ = ___

2. 12 buttons divided among 4 cups.

   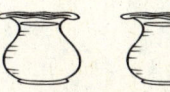 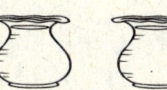  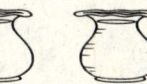

   ___ ÷ ___ = ___

3. 15 flowers divided among 5 vases.

   🏺 🏺 🏺 🏺 🏺

   ___ ÷ ___ = ___

4. 8 balls divided among 2 cartons.

   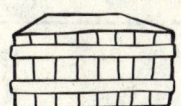 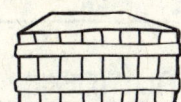

   ___ ÷ ___ = ___

Problem Solving *Reasonableness*

Draw a picture to help answer the question.

5. Rita has 14 cat treats.
   She has 3 cats.
   How many treats will each cat get?
   Are there any treats left over?

   _____

   _____

Use with Lesson 12-8. **157**

PROBLEM-SOLVING SKILL

P 12-9

Choose an Operation

Circle the number sentence that solves the problem.

1. Sara makes 6 bracelets. She puts 3 beads on each bracelet. How many beads does she use in all?

   $6 - 3 = 3$ $\qquad$ $6 + 3 = 9$ $\qquad$ $6 \times 3 = 18$

   Sara uses _____ beads.

2. Monty builds a birdhouse. He uses 7 pieces of wood for the house and 3 pieces of wood for the roof. How many pieces of wood does he use in all?

   $7 + 3 = 10$ $\qquad$ $7 \times 3 = 21$ $\qquad$ $7 - 3 = 4$

   Monty uses _____ pieces of wood.

3. Mr. Kaplan bakes 8 muffins. He eats 2 muffins for breakfast. How many muffins are left?

   $8 \times 2 = 16$ $\qquad$ $8 - 2 = 6$ $\qquad$ $8 + 4 = 12$

   Mr. Kaplan has _____ muffins left.

4. Miss Thomas sews 5 dolls. She has 15 buttons. She wants to sew the same number of buttons on each doll. How many buttons does each doll get?

   $5 + 3 = 8$ $\qquad$ $15 \div 5 = 3$ $\qquad$ $5 - 3 = 2$

   Each doll gets _____ buttons.

PROBLEM-SOLVING APPLICATIONS

P 12-10

Up, Up, and Away!

Solve.

1. A plane has 6 rows of seats in one part of the cabin. Each row has 3 seats. How many seats are there in all?

   _____ rows × _____ seats in each row = _____ seats in all

2. Javier brought magazines to read on the plane. It took Javier 2 hours to read each magazine. The flight lasted 6 hours. How many magazines did Javier read during the flight?

   _____ ÷ _____ = _____ magazines

3. A passenger has two suitcases. One suitcase weighs 27 pounds. The other suitcase weighs 56 pounds. How many pounds do the two suitcases weigh in all?

   _____ + _____ = _____ pounds in all

Writing in Math

4. Write a multiplication story about a trip you would like to take on an airplane.

   _____

   _____

   _____

Use with Lesson 12-10.